AMERICAN
COUNTRY
CHRISTMAS

Book Four

COMPILED AND EDITED BY
Brenda Waldron Kolb
and Shannon Sexton Jernigan

Oxmoor
House®

Library of Congress Catalog Number: 94-65471
ISBN: 0-8487-1444-X
ISSN: 1074-8946
Manufactured in the United States of America
First Printing

Editor-in-Chief: Nancy Fitzpatrick Wyatt
Senior Homes Editor: Mary Kay Culpepper
Senior Foods Editor: Susan Carlisle Payne
Senior Editor, Editorial Services: Olivia Kindig Wells
Art Director: James Boone

AMERICAN COUNTRY CHRISTMAS BOOK FOUR

Editor: Brenda Waldron Kolb
Assistant Editor: Shannon Sexton Jernigan
Editorial Assistant: Laura A. Fredericks
Copy Editor: Susan Smith Cheatham
Copy Assistant: Jennifer K. Mathews
Assistant Art Director: Cynthia R. Cooper
Senior Designer: Melissa M. Clark
Senior Photographer: John O'Hagan
Photographer: Ralph Anderson
Photo Stylists: Katie Stoddard, Virginia R. Cravens
Production and Distribution Director: Phillip Lee
Associate Production Manager: Theresa L. Beste
Production Assistant: Marianne Jordan Wilson
Artist: Kelly Davis
Senior Production Designer: Larry Hunter
Publishing Systems Administrator: Rick Tucker
Test Kitchen Home Economist: Elizabeth Tyler Luckett
Recipe Editor: Lisa Hooper Talley
Recipe Copy Editor: Donna Baldone

FRONT COVER, clockwise from top: star ornament, page 19; tree candle holder, page 20; velvet frame, page 115; birdhouse, page 9; soap and bath oils, page 124; mittens, page 82; velvet ornaments, page 115.
BACK COVER, clockwise from top left: garland, page 10; Triple-Treat Bars, page 91; tree for the birds, page 133; pinecone fire starters, page 136; birdhouse (center), page 9.

DEAR READERS,

The more the merrier, runs one old saying. Less is more, goes another.

For this edition of *American Country Christmas,* we aim for something in between—more projects and recipes, but ones that take less time and money.

That's how we put the plan to our designers and recipe developers. Busy people all, they liked the idea of revving things up while paring things down.

They cut materials lists and weighed costs against benefits. They suggested alternatives and timesaving tips. They chose holiday themes and materials with year-round appeal. In short, they had a great time pitting their creativity against the test of practicality.

The result? We believe it's our strongest collection yet. You'll find dozens of great-looking crafts and decorations. The gift foods and menus for easy entertaining will make mouths water. And the best part is, each project and recipe makes wise use of your valuable resources.

After all, Christmas comes but once a year. With this edition of *American Country Christmas* as your guide, plan on a season of crafting and cooking—and enjoying every minute of it.

The Editors

Instructions for birdhouse are on page 9.

COUNTRY CHRISTMAS AT HOME

Decorating for the holidays is a wonderful way to feather your nest—and our collection of seasonal projects proves the point. For starters, you can build this birdhouse. It looks great year-round, but it's a natural at Christmas.

PERCHES WITH PERFECT PITCH

For birdhouse collectors on your list, these mossy lodges will strike
just the right note. And because the materials are so inexpensive,
you'll be able to make a whole village for a song.

Materials for 1 birdhouse:

Patterns on page 154

Tracing paper

Matboard pieces: for small birdhouse, 1 (7" x 11") piece, 2 (6") squares for roof, 1 (5⅞" x 4½") piece for floor; for large birdhouse, 1 (9" x 13") piece, 2 (8") squares for roof, 1 (7⅞" x 6") piece for floor

Craft knife

Hot-glue gun and glue sticks

Masking tape

Waxed paper

2 paintbrushes

Clear-drying craft glue

Birdseed

Florist's moss

Twigs in similar diameters for perch

Red acrylic paint

Sticks in similar diameters for roof trim: for small birdhouse, 5 (6"-long) sticks; for large birdhouse, 5 (8"-long) sticks

Note: Birdhouse is for indoor, decorative use only.

1. Transfer patterns and cut out. Using tracing paper, transfer patterns to 7" x 11" piece of matboard (for small birdhouse) or 9" x 13" piece of matboard (for large birdhouse) and cut out with craft knife. Cut opening from front only. Hot-glue chimney pieces together, securing with small strips of masking tape.

2. Assemble frame. Referring to Diagram, hot-glue front and back pieces to floor, securing with small strips of tape. Hot-glue roof pieces to sides, allowing equal amount of overhang for eaves at front and back. Secure with small strips of tape.

3. Add chimney. Glue chimney to right side of roof as indicated. Secure with small strips of tape.

4. Cover birdhouse. Cover work surface with waxed paper. Using paintbrush, coat chimney and front and back pieces with craft glue. Sprinkle with birdseed, covering entire surface. Glue moss on roof. Let dry.

5. Make perch. Cut 2 twigs equal to width of opening. Cut 4 or 5 (2"-long) twigs. Referring to Diagram, hot-glue long twigs on top of short twigs. Paint perch red; let dry. Glue 1 short end of perch to bottom of birdhouse opening as indicated.

6. Trim roof. Referring to photograph, hot-glue 6" or 8" sticks to roof edges, trimming sticks as necessary to fit.

DIAGRAM

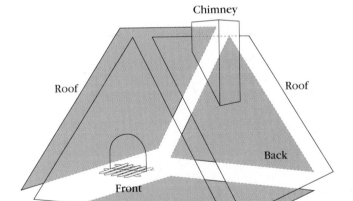

SEASONABLE REQUESTS

For Chris Goddard, an Arkansas designer with a reputation for fresh, natural decorations, Christmas really begins in October.

That's when clients start calling Beauregard, Chris's shop in Fayetteville, to get on Chris's holiday schedule.

As the season nears, the pace intensifies. Last Christmas, Chris and his staff of 14 decorated 178 homes—an average of 3 or 4 a day. Chris smiles when he recalls that, amid the hubbub, he never got around to decorating his own home for the holidays.

At 26, Chris may be young, but he's no stranger to the business. "Nearly everyone in my family is a florist or interior designer," he says. He needn't look far for inspiration; his uncle, Leonard Tharp, was a prominent floral designer whose clients included Nancy Reagan.

After graduating from the University of Arkansas with degrees in both design and business, Chris worked his floral wizardry out of his home for two years before opening Beauregard "on the square" in Fayetteville. (See page 156 for more information on Chris's shop.)

Since then, success has been sweet and calendars crowded. Chris says, "We take a simple, naturalistic approach to our designs"—a technique clients clearly appreciate. But floral design isn't the only thing they come for: Beauregard also offers home furnishings as well as entertaining and interior design services, all with Chris's signature flair.

His casual, close-to-the-earth style is evident in the garland that graces the door shown at left. The garland, which is best suited for a covered or protected entryway, features components that can be used year after year. To learn how he created it, just turn the page.

A Garland to Ring In the Holidays

These materials and instructions are for the garland shown on the preceding pages.

Vines and an evergreen garland in 25' lengths will be ample for most doors; yours may need more or less yardage. To order raffia, an evergreen garland, the decorative birdhouses, or garden angel shown in the photograph, see the source listings on page 156.

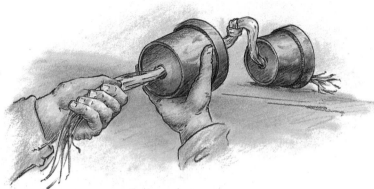

1 Make bells. If desired, use gold paint pen to decorate flowerpots with stars, moons, or other simple designs. For each of 6 small bells, knot 1 end of 1 raffia bundle; thread other end through 4" pot and knot. Thread raffia through 6" pot; knot again. For 6 large bells, repeat procedure with remaining pots.

Materials:
Terra-cotta flowerpots: 6 (4"), 12 (6"),
   6 (8")
Gold paint pen (optional)
25'–30' (total) raffia (about 3 packages),
   separated into 12 bundles of 10–15
   strands each (reserve remaining strands)
8–10 bunches wheat stalks
Florist's wire
1 dozen dried sunflower blooms
   (or dried hydrangea blooms)
5 large cup hooks
25' grapevine and/or honeysuckle vine
   for garland base
25' evergreen garland
Assorted holiday greenery

4 Hang garland around door.
Screw cup hooks into door frame, 1 at top and 2 on each side. Using florist's wire, attach vine to cup hooks. Wrap evergreen garland around vine, securing with raffia. If desired, tuck in cuttings of assorted greenery.

2 **Make wheat sheaves.** To make each of 10 sheaves, fan 20–30 wheat stalks and secure with florist's wire two-thirds from stalk ends. Trim stalk ends even. Cover wire with raffia, or hold 4 wheat stalks together as 1 and tie around wire.

3 **Assemble garland centerpiece.** In 1 hand, gather 1 wheat sheaf, 3–5 dried sunflowers, and 2 raffia bundles of small bells; with other hand, tightly wrap florist's wire around centerpiece. Add 1 large bell; wrap with wire. Cover wire with raffia.

5 **Add bells.** Referring to photograph on preceding pages for placement, attach centerpiece to top of garland, securing centerpiece with florist's wire. To attach each remaining bell, tie excess raffia at top of bell to sides of garland.

6 **Add wheat sheaves and raffia.** Referring to photograph for placement, tie wheat sheaves to garland with strands of raffia or stems of knotted wheat stalks. To fill in gaps, weave loose bundles of remaining raffia into garland.

Seeing Stars

Gather a purchased twig swag, fabric scraps, and a few other materials—then make this rustic accent in a twinkling.

Materials:
Patterns on page 155
Tracing paper
2 (9" x 12") pieces white
   cotton fabric
Dressmaker's pen
Thin batting or fleece
White thread
Small paintbrush
Gold fabric paint
1 package 60"-long natural raffia
Purchased 3'-wide twig swag
Hot-glue gun and glue sticks
Florist's wire
Gold glitter fabric paint

1. Make stars. Using tracing paper, transfer 6 star patterns to 1 fabric piece. Stack plain fabric piece, batting, and marked fabric piece (marked side up); pin. Topstitch outline of each star in 1 continuous seam, pivoting needle at points. Cut out each star just outside stitching line. Using paintbrush, randomly daub gold fabric paint on 1 side of each star, applying more paint at edges; let dry.

2. Assemble swag. Wind bundle of 10 raffia strands around bottom of swag and glue to secure. Tie remaining strands into large bow, using florist's wire to secure. Glue bow to center of swag. Randomly daub swag and raffia with gold paint and gold glitter paint. Referring to photograph for placement, glue stars to swag.

Quick Tips

• For no-sew stars, omit the batting and substitute paper-backed fusible web. Follow the manufacturer's instructions to fuse the two pieces of fabric together.

• Make your own swag with fresh grapevines or honey-suckle vines. Cut pliable lengths about 2'- to 3'-long. Hot-glue 2 or 3 vines together for the base. Bend several shorter lengths to make a center arch and 2 smaller side arches. Secure the arches with hot glue, florist's wire, or small nails.

• Instead of making a raffia bow, purchase a premade one.

• Display your swag on a pegged shelf; over a door frame, headboard, mantel, or painting; or outdoors in a breezeway or porch that's protected from the elements.

ART FOR THE HEARTH

Designer Molly Pritchett created this stenciled hearth rug especially for beginners. The rug is small, its geometric design is easily reproducible, and it requires only three paint colors.

Materials:
Patterns and diagrams on pages 138–39
Black fine-tipped permanent marker
3 (8½" x 11") sheets frosted template plastic
Craft knife
42" x 32" piece heavyweight cotton canvas
Thick craft glue
Steam iron
2" foam brush
Acrylic gesso
150-grit sandpaper
Green latex paint
Acrylic paints: metallic silver, metallic copper
2 stencil brushes
¾"-wide masking tape
Clear quick-drying oil varnish

1. Make stencils. Using black marker, trace stencil patterns onto frosted side of plastic. For star design, Stencil 1 is for silver paint and Stencil 2 is for copper paint. For inner border, Stencils 3–5 are for silver and copper paint. Using craft knife, cut stencils on shiny side of plastic. Use clear tape to correct cutting errors. Set stencils aside.

2. Prepare canvas. To hem canvas, turn under 1" on all sides and glue to back. Lay canvas facedown on flat surface. Steam-iron back, removing wrinkles and squaring corners; let dry completely. Using foam brush, apply 1 coat of gesso to back; let dry.

Turn canvas over and steam-iron front. Apply 2 coats gesso, letting each coat dry completely. Lightly sand front and wipe clean.

3. Paint canvas. Using foam brush, apply 2 coats of green paint to front, letting each coat dry completely. Turn canvas over and apply 2 more coats to hem.

4. Stencil star design. Referring to Diagram 1 on page 138, use a pencil and yardstick to mark guidelines. Beginning in center, align holes at corners of Stencil 1 with intersections of guidelines. Using silver paint, stencil star and lines with Stencil 1. Referring to Diagram 2 on page 138, repeat to fill in remaining areas. Let dry. Beginning in center and using copper paint, stencil circles and star facets with Stencil 2 in same manner. Let dry.

5. Stencil inner border. Using Stencils 3–5 as indicated on Diagram 2, stencil inner border. Let dry.

6. Stencil outer border. Place a strip of masking tape just outside each edge of inner border. Measure ¾" from tape and place another strip of tape. Using copper paint, stencil outer border between 2 lines of tape. Let dry and remove tape.

7. Apply finish. Using foam brush, apply varnish; let dry. Sand lightly and wipe clean. Repeat to apply 2 more layers of varnish.

A Rug Renaissance

In the decade since Molly began making floorcloths, she's noticed a trend. While floorcloths as a craft may be traditional, today their designs are often anything but.

Floorcloths were popular in the eighteenth and nineteenth centuries, and Molly's first pieces were historical reproductions for museums. But as the rug revival caught on, artists began emphasizing creation over re-creation.

These days Molly's designs include folk art, faux finishes, the sedately classical to the brazenly contemporary. The important thing is not what worked then, but what works now. (For information on Molly's floorcloths, see page 156.)

PRECIOUS METALS

Look in craft stores and hobby shops for shiny craft metal—
the secret to making these tooled beauties. The paper-thin, flexible sheets come
in a variety of colors; we chose copper for its warm, mellow glow. In any hue,
the fun is in the crafting: embossing and shaping the metal
into ornaments, candle holders, and frames.

Ornaments

Materials for 1 ornament:
Pattern on page 140
Tracing paper
1 (6" x 10") piece 36-gauge copper craft metal
Embossing tool: dry ballpoint pen, orange stick,
   or other tool with dull point
Punching tool: punching awl, ice pick, or other
   tool with sharp point
Epoxy resin
Scrap of silk cording

1. Transfer pattern. Using tracing paper, transfer desired pattern to metal. Using scissors, cut out 2 along outlines.

2. For tree, emboss design. Place metal (dull side up) on flat, padded surface. Place pattern on top of metal. Using ruler to steady embossing tool and working in 1 direction, trace design lines, pressing gently to emboss metal. Use punching tool to make holes where indicated.

3. For star, crimp points. Beginning at base of each point and working toward tip, fold metal accordion style (see Diagram).

4. Fit pieces together. Make a vertical 2¼"-long cut from top down on 1 piece and from bottom up on remaining piece. With pieces at right angles, interlock pieces along cut lines to form 3-dimensional shape. Glue along cut lines to secure.

5. Make hanger. With punching tool, punch small hole in top of 1 piece. Thread cording through hole and knot ends together.

DIAGRAM

Step 1

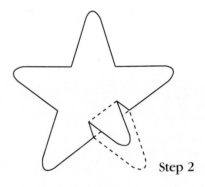

Step 2

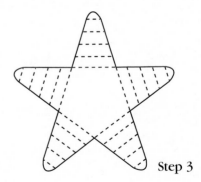

Step 3

Candle Holders

Materials for 1 candle holder:
Pattern on page 140
Tracing paper
Votive candle
1 (12" x 13") piece 36-gauge copper craft metal
Embossing tool: dry ballpoint pen, orange stick, or other tool with dull point
Punching tool: punching awl, ice pick, or other tool with sharp point (for tree)
Epoxy resin
3 small pebbles

1. Transfer pattern. Using tracing paper, trace desired pattern and cut out.

Place metal (dull side up) on flat, padded surface. Center candle on metal. Using sharp pencil, lightly trace around base of candle. Set candle aside.

Referring to Diagram, transfer pattern to perimeter of circle 3 times, spacing designs evenly.

2. For tree, emboss design. Place pattern on top of metal. Using ruler to steady embossing tool and working in 1 direction, trace design, pressing gently to emboss metal. Use punching tool to make holes where indicated. Using scissors, cut out along outside edges.

3. For star, crimp points. Using scissors, cut out along outside edges. To crimp points, see Step 3 for Ornaments (page 19).

4. Finish candle holder. Bend designs up to form sides of votive holder. Glue pebbles to bottom of holder, placing 1 pebble under each design. Place candle in center of holder.

DIAGRAM

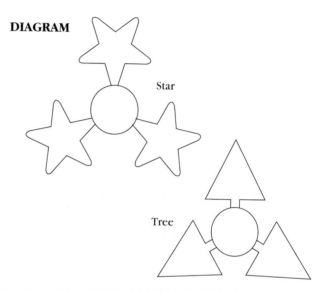

Star

Tree

Frame

Materials:
Pattern on page 140
Tracing paper
Colored pencils: red, black
1 (12" x 13") piece 36-gauge copper
    craft metal
1 precut 8" x 10" photo mat with
    3½" x 5½" opening
Masking tape
Embossing tool: dry ballpoint pen, orange stick,
    or other tool with dull point
1 (8" x 10") mirror, photograph, or print
Epoxy resin
1 (8" x 10") piece felt for backing

1. Transfer pattern. Using colored pencils and tracing paper, trace pattern and cut out.

Place metal (shiny side up) on flat, padded surface. Center mat on metal. Using sharp pencil, lightly trace around outside edge of mat and inside mat opening to mark frame front. Set mat aside.

Center pattern (right side up) inside markings for frame front. Tape pattern in place.

2. Emboss design. Using ruler to steady embossing tool and working in 1 direction, trace along solid black lines, pressing gently to emboss metal.

Turn metal over. Center pattern (right side down) inside markings for frame front and tape in place. Trace along red lines, making a slightly heavier impression than before to create relief in design.

3. Make frame. Using scissors, cut out opening in center of frame front, leaving 1" extra inside embossed edges. Clip inside corners up to embossed edges. Place metal (shiny side up) on mat, aligning embossed edges of frame front with edges of mat. Fold inside edge of frame front to wrong side of mat.

4. Frame mirror. Lay frame right side down; place mirror, right side down, on frame; align edges. Wrap excess edges of metal to back of mirror, trimming and overlapping at corners to lie flat. Glue metal to mirror back. Center and glue felt piece on mirror back.

Tooling Around

As the owner of The Magic Factory in Rome, Georgia, Kay Clark designs, makes, and markets decorative accessories fashioned from different types of metals. She designed the candle holders and ornaments featured on the preceding pages, and she offers these tips for working with craft metal:

• **On the cutting edge.** The edges of sheets of craft metal are sharp, so protect your hands by wearing gloves or covering the metal edges with strips of masking tape.

• **Gauge the outcome.** Craft metal comes in a variety of gauges, or thicknesses. Kay recommends using 36-gauge craft metal, which is thin enough to be cut with scissors and easily shaped but thick enough to hold up well for most craft projects.

• **Flying colors.** Craft metal is available in a variety of shades: copper (as called for in the projects on the preceding pages), gold, silver (or aluminum), even blue and red. Consider using different colors to achieve a different look.

• **Mellow out.** Craft metal has a shiny, highly reflective finish. To antique it, simply wipe it with vinegar.

• **Use a soft touch.** When you emboss designs on craft metal, always work on a flat, padded surface, which has enough "give" for the embossing tool to make a good impression on the metal. A stack of newspapers or old magazines does the job nicely.

• **Go to the source.** Craft metal is widely available at craft stores and hobby shops. To order craft metal by mail, turn to the source listing on page 156.

A BANNER SANTA

**Flag the attention of passersby with this pink-cheeked, bright-eyed elf.
Stitched from nylon flag fabric, your bold banner will sail through
many winters to come.**

Materials:
60"-wide nylon flag fabric: ⅝ yard green; ½
  yard each red, white, and ecru; ⅛ yard each
  dark pink, light pink, black, and gold (see
  Note below)
Liquid ravel preventer (optional)
Thread to match fabrics
¼"-diameter grommet and applicator
Appliqué scissors (optional)

Note: Nylon flag fabric and flagpoles are available at fabric stores and from the source listed on page 156.

1. Cut fabrics. From green, cut a 22" x 33" piece for top. From red, cut a 16" x 33" piece for bottom and a right triangle measuring 11" x 21" x 23¼".

From white, cut the following: 1 (2¼" x 12½") piece for hat fur, rounding corners slightly; 2 (2½" x 7½") pieces for hair; 1 (13" x 16") piece for beard; and 2 (5" x 10") pieces for mustache. For hair and beard pieces, cut waves along edges. For mustache pieces, referring to photograph, cut pieces into same-size crescents.

From ecru, cut a 14½"-diameter circle for face. From dark pink, cut a 2¼"-diameter circle for mouth and a 4"-diameter circle for nose. From light pink, cut 2 (4½"-diameter) circles for cheeks. From black, cut 2 (3½"-diameter) circles for eyes. From gold, cut a 3½"-diameter circle for bell. If desired, apply liquid ravel preventer to all raw edges; let dry.

2. Stitch background. Overlap 1 long edge of green piece on 1 long edge of large red piece ½"; baste. Using red thread, stitch pieces together with narrow zigzag. Trim seam allowance. Using medium satin stitch, stitch over narrow zigzag, encasing raw edges.

Turn bottom edge under ¼" and then 1"; press. Repeat on sides. Using matching thread, edgestitch along first fold and again along outside edge.

3. Make casing for flagpole. At top edge, turn under ½" and then 3¼"; press. With right side down, find top left corner. Unfold casing. Following manufacturer's instructions, attach grommet in side hem beside crease. (Grommet will receive lacing on flagpole to hold banner in place.) Refold casing and edgestitch casing in place; topstitch ¼" from edgestitching.

4. Pin appliqué pieces in place. Referring to photograph for placement, arrange and securely pin appliqué pieces on background in the following order: face, hair, hat (with shortest edge on face and hair, and tip above top edge of banner), hat fur, eyes, cheeks, nose, beard, mouth, and mustache. Fold top of hat down so that fold aligns with bottom of casing and tip points downward. Place bell over tip of hat. Adjust pieces as desired.

5. Stitch appliqué pieces. Using matching thread, stitch outline of each piece with narrow zigzag. For hat, stitch all raw edges and fold. Using appliqué scissors if desired, trim background fabric from behind pieces. If desired, apply liquid ravel preventer to raw edges on banner back; let dry. Using matching thread, stitch over narrow zigzag with medium satin stitch, encasing all raw edges.

6. Add details. Referring to photograph for placement, use black thread and medium satin stitch to stitch openings in bell and speckles in hat fur. Use white thread and medium satin stitch to stitch gleams in eyes and waves in hair, mustache, and beard.

SHE GIVES SOFA PILLOWS THE SLIP

Peggy Ann Williams piles up pillow slipcovers that can update a sofa or a whole room. Work one or more of her designs in red or green fabrics, and you'll have ever-stylish pillows that look especially festive at Christmas.

The following instructions will enable you to slipcover a pillow of any size. Wash and press all fabrics before cutting. For information on ordering the stripe and check fabrics, see page 156. All seam allowances are ½".

Lace Up a Pacesetter

Materials for 1 slipcover:
Pillow or pillow form
Fabric (see Step 1); thread to match
Interfacing
Dressmaker's pen
⅜"-diameter grommets and applicator
⅜" cotton cable cording

  1. Cut fabric. Measure length and width of pillow and add 5" to each. Cut 2 fabric pieces to match.
  2. Interface edges. Cut 8 (2"-wide) strips of interfacing. Following manufacturer's instructions, apply interfacing to wrong side of each edge.

25

3. Finish edges. Turn under ½" and then 2" along all edges, mitering corners; press and baste. Topstitch ½" and then 1½" from each edge.

4. Add trims. Mark placement for grommets 1" from edges and 1½" apart. Attach grommets. Insert pillow. Lace together with cording, tying a knot or bow at each corner.

Magic Miters

Materials for 1 slipcover:
Square pillow or pillow form
Tracing paper
Stripe fabric (see steps 1 and 2); thread to match
Lining fabric
1" buttons

1. Make pattern. Measure width of pillow and add 6". From tracing paper, cut a square this size. Fold in half diagonally twice. Unfold and cut out 1 quarter-square triangle along fold lines.

2. Cut fabric. Cut 8 triangles from fabric, adding seam allowances and aligning pattern in same place on fabric so stripes will match.

3. Piece front and back. For front, join 4 triangles to form a square, matching stripes. Repeat for back.

4. Line front and back. From lining fabric, cut 2 squares to match front and back. With right sides facing and raw edges aligned, stitch front and lining together, leaving an opening for turning. Clip corners and turn; slipstitch opening closed. Repeat for back.

5. Attach buttons. On right side of front, mark and stitch buttonholes 1½" from each edge. On wrong side of back, mark placement and sew on buttons. Insert pillow. Button closed.

Fringe Benefits

Materials for 1 slipcover:
Rectangular pillow or pillow form
Fabric (see Step 1); thread to match
Dressmaker's pen
1" buttons
3" cotton bullion fringe for sides

1. Cut fabric. For back, measure length and width of pillow and add 1" to each. Cut 1 fabric piece to match. For front, measure length of pillow and add 4½". Measure width of pillow and add 1". Cut 1 fabric piece to match.

2. Cut front. On right side of front, measure and mark center of long top and bottom edges of fabric. On bottom edge, measure 5" to left of center and mark A; on top edge, measure 2½" to right of center and mark B. Mark diagonal line connecting A and B; cut along marked line, dividing front into 2 pieces.

3. Stitch front. On left front, mark and stitch buttonholes 1½" from diagonal edge. Turn each diagonal edge under ½"; topstitch. With right sides up, overlap diagonal edges of left over right 1½"; baste.

4. Add fringe to front. Measure sides. Cut fringe to match. With right sides facing, edges aligned, and fringe toward center of fabric, stitch fringe to sides.

5. Stitch slipcover and add buttons. With right sides facing and raw edges aligned, stitch front to back. Trim seams and corners; turn through diagonal opening. Topstitch ¼" from top and bottom edges to simulate piping. Insert pillow. On right front, mark placement for buttons. Stitch buttons. Button closed.

Button Down a Wraparound

Materials for 1 slipcover:
Pillow or pillow form
Fabric (see Step 1); thread to match
Dressmaker's pen
1 (1½") shank covered-button form
1½"-wide cotton eyelash fringe

   1. Cut fabric. Measure length of pillow and add 1". Measure width of pillow, multiply by 2½, and add 3". Cut fabric to these measurements.

   2. Mark fold lines. Fold 1 short edge under ½" and topstitch. To mark first fold line: On wrong side, beginning at bottom hemmed edge, measure width of pillow and mark. To mark second fold line: Beginning at first fold line, measure width of pillow and mark.

   3. Stitch slipcover. With right sides facing, fold fabric up along first fold line, aligning hemmed edge with second fold line. Stitch side seams between fold lines. Turn. Topstitch ¼" from each side edge to simulate piping. On flap, turn each edge under ½" and topstitch.

   4. Add fringe and button. Trim fringe to fit long edge of flap and topstitch in place. Cover button form with fabric scrap. In center of flap, mark and stitch

buttonhole 1" from fringe. Insert pillow. Fold flap down. Mark placement and sew on button. Button closed.

Top It Off with a Tassel

Materials for 1 slipcover:
Pillow or pillow form
Fabric (see Step 1); thread to match
Dressmaker's pen
Tracing paper
1" button
3" tassel

   1. Cut fabric and mark fold lines. Repeat steps 1 and 2 for "Button Down a Wraparound."

   2. Prepare flap. Mark center of short raw edge. Using ruler, mark a line from center mark to each raw edge at second fold line. Cut fabric along lines, adding seam allowances.

   For lining: Use tracing paper to trace outline of flap. Add 1" along bottom edge and cut out. Using pattern, cut out lining; overcast long edge.

   3. Stitch slipcover. With right sides facing and short raw edges aligned, stitch lining to flap, leaving overcast edge open. Turn flap. Repeat Step 3 of "Button Down a Wraparound" to fold and stitch side seams. Turn. Topstitch ¼" from each side edge and along point of flap to simulate piping.

   4. Add button and tassel. Mark and stitch buttonhole 2" from point. Insert pillow. Fold flap down. Mark and sew on button. Sew tassel to flap. Button closed.

IDEAS
STYLE BY THE YARD

This swath of sheer fabric with finger-painted polka dots may be the season's quickest, most versatile decoration. The hardest part will be deciding just where you're going to use it.

One-Stop Shopping

Head to the fabric store for the three items you'll need to make your own style by the yard. Our version required 7 yards of 60"-wide sheer white polyester fabric—the kind used for making drapery sheers. You may choose to buy more or fewer yards or fabric of a narrower width.

You will also need 2 (1-ounce) bottles of acrylic fabric paint—1 each of gold and silver. We used DecoArt™ So-Soft Metallics in Imperial Gold and Silver Platinum.

Do the Polka

Wash and dry the fabric, omitting fabric softener. Cover your work surface with newspaper or kraft paper. Using the tip of your index finger, randomly finger-paint gold and silver polka dots on the fabric. If desired, repeat to give each polka dot another coat. Let dry.

Deck the Halls

For a snowdrift of a tree skirt, simply pool the fabric around the base of the tree. For a romantic table scarf, curve the length down the center of a table.

Other possibilities include draping it across the mantel, wrapping it around an evergreen garland on a staircase, or overlaying it on a plain white tablecloth.

Table scarf

Tree skirt

Instructions for wreath are on page 33.

HOLIDAY HANDIWORK

For decorations, gifts, and the sheer joy of expressing yourself, there's nothing like creating projects perfect for Christmas. When you craft a birch-bark wreath, for instance, you put yourself in the holiday spirit—and you do the same for all who come calling.

A WOODSY, WELCOMING WREATH

**Deck your door with a rustic wreath fashioned from birch-bark tubes.
Mother Nature supplies the appealing colors and textures;
all you need to add is a bow.**

Materials:
15" flat-back Styrofoam wreath
18" square kraft paper
Craft glue
18" length 26-gauge wire
Wire cutters
5 (12") tubes purchased birch bark (see Note below)
Hot-glue gun and glue sticks
2½ yards 2"-wide gingham wire ribbon

Note: For birch bark or for birch-bark paper (which can be used as a substitute for real bark), see source listings on page 156.

1. Cover wreath back. Place wreath in center of kraft paper. Referring to Diagram 1, measure and mark a circle 2" from outer edge of wreath; repeat for inner edge. Cut paper along marked lines. Using craft glue, glue foam wreath, flat side down, in center of paper circle. Referring to Diagram 2, clip excess paper up to wreath edges at 2" intervals. Fold cut sections to front of wreath and glue.

2. Make hanger. Wrap wire around wreath from front to back at top center. Twist wire to form a loop, trimming excess.

3. Cover wreath front. Referring to Diagram 3, cut tubes of birch bark into 3" x 6" sections. Hot-glue 1 bark piece to front of wreath, aligning outer edge of bark with outer edge of wreath. Continue gluing bark pieces in this manner, slightly overlapping edges, to cover wreath front. Trim excess bark along edges.

4. Add bow. Tie a 10-loop bow from gingham ribbon. Glue or tie bow to top center of wreath.

DIAGRAM 1

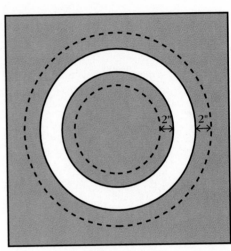

DIAGRAM 2

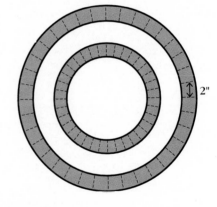

DIAGRAM 3

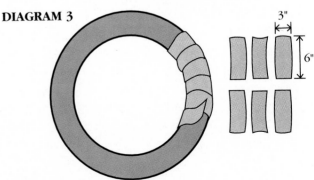

33

Presents from Papier-Mâché

Give a traditional craft a new twist with stylized designs in bright colors.
Begin with a sturdy base, such as a tray or bowl, and follow our
easy instructions for building a papier-mâché work of art.

Papier-mâché Pointers

•Papier-mâché can be done with many different types of paper. However, we found that kraft paper or grocery bags provide a sturdy base with few layers.

•For easy removal, use petroleum jelly to coat the inside of the item you're using as a mold; then line the mold with plastic wrap. (Omit this step for the tray.)

•Prepare strips by tearing the paper as shown below. Always tear the paper; cut edges do not blend in well.

•Mix the adhesive, following the manufacturer's instructions. You will need approximately 2 cups of adhesive mixture for each of these projects. Allow the mixture to sit for several minutes until it is the consistency of jelly. Coat each paper strip as you are ready to use it, dipping it in the adhesive and pulling it between your fingers to remove excess.

•To form the papier-mâché base, layer strips 1 at a time on 1 side of the object until the entire surface is covered. Take care to smooth each strip, leaving no air or lumps of adhesive trapped between the layers. Let dry completely. Carefully lift the paper shape from the mold. Add additional layers of paper on both the inside and the outside of the shape. To give the piece more strength and to aid in counting the layers, alternate the direction of the strips for each layer. Let each layer dry before adding the next one. You will need at least 5 layers for a sturdy finished project.

•If you live in a humid climate, the papier-mâché may air-dry slowly. To aid the drying process, place the papier-mâché shape in a 200° oven and check it every 30 minutes until it dries.

•You can store leftover adhesive mixture in an airtight container in the refrigerator for up to 3 weeks.

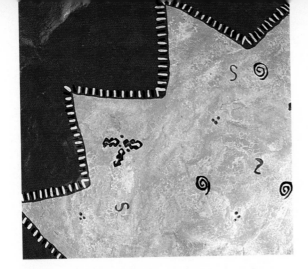

Bowl

Materials:
Patterns on page 141
Vinyl wallcovering adhesive
Mixing bowl and spoon
1 roll kraft paper or 5 brown grocery bags
   (with no printing)
Glass or metal bowl with rim for mold
Petroleum jelly
Plastic wrap
Acrylic paints: sandstone, ivory, red, green, black
Paintbrushes
Sponge
Tracing paper
Matte varnish

1. Prepare materials. Mix adhesive and tear paper as described in Papier-mâché Pointers.

2. Cover bowl. Coat inside of bowl with petroleum jelly. Cover with plastic wrap, overlapping edges.

3. Build layers. Layer adhesive-coated paper strips inside bowl, allowing paper strips to extend beyond top edge 1½" to form rim. Let dry. Carefully remove paper from bowl. Add at least 4 additional layers of paper, 2 on inside and 2 on outside of paper bowl form. Let dry between layers.

4. Paint base coat. Paint entire bowl sandstone. Let dry. Using sponge, add ivory accents.

5. Paint details. Referring to photograph on page 35, lightly draw zigzag points inside bowl. Using tracing paper, transfer holly patterns to bowl. Referring to photograph for colors, paint designs. Let dry.

6. Apply varnish. Finish bowl with 2 coats of matte varnish. Let dry between coats.

Tray

Materials:
Patterns on page 141
Vinyl wallcovering adhesive
Mixing bowl and spoon
1 roll kraft paper or 8 brown grocery bags
   (with no printing)
Tray with rim
Acrylic paints: sandstone, ivory, red, green, black
Paintbrushes
Sponge
Tracing paper
Matte varnish

1. Prepare materials. Mix adhesive and tear paper as described in Papier-mâché Pointers.

2. Enclose tray. Layer adhesive-coated paper strips directly onto tray until entire tray is enclosed. Let dry. Continue layering until desired thickness is achieved.

3. Paint base coat. Paint entire tray sandstone. Let dry. Using sponge, add ivory accents.

4. Paint details. Referring to photograph on pages 34–35, lightly draw zigzag points around tray. Using tracing paper, transfer reindeer and holly patterns to tray as desired. Referring to photograph for colors, paint designs. Let dry.

5. Apply varnish. Finish tray with 2 coats of matte varnish. Let dry between coats.

HEAVENLY HOST

Folk artist Nancy Thomas is well known for her Santas, snowmen, and other pieces. But her fans seem fondest of her celestial choirs.

Visitors to Nancy's gallery in Yorktown, Virginia, meet their first angel on the sign out front. Over the door to her adjacent studio hovers a second seraph.

Within, winged creatures, stars, suns, and moons beckon. Large, small, and in between, they're crafted of painted wood, tin, and ceramics. Most don't remain there long, Nancy admits. At the gallery's Christmas open house, held annually the weekend before Thanksgiving, they're always her best-sellers.

Nancy's imagination and paintbrush are by no means stirred only by celestial themes. Her rustic Statue of Liberty was commissioned by the Museum of American Folk Art in New York, and her carved animals have trimmed the White House Christmas tree. She recently completed for Colonial Williamsburg a series of six-foot paintings of Saint Nicholas; the bearded fellow peeking over Nancy's shoulder in the photograph above depicts Santa in the early 1900s.

But one always returns to Nancy's more ethereal subjects. Fifteen years ago, her angels were among the first of her works to attract the notice of collectors, gallery owners, and even Hollywood set designers (a bevy of them appeared in the movie *Tootsie*). Today her cherubs remain popular. "In fact," says Nancy, "without my really intending it, guardian angels have become my trademark."

Nancy later began creating the suns, moons, and stars that spangle her collection. It's hard to imagine now a world where heavenly bodies didn't crowd stores' shelves, but Nancy's versions are original, compelling—clearly a cut above.

That fact can only be attributed to Nancy's distinctive style. Quirky rather than cute, more sanguine than

sentimental, her work blends the traditional and the strictly personal. She combines historical motifs with contemporary design elements, and she isn't afraid to treat time-honored themes with humor. (To find out more about Nancy's work, see the source listing on page 156.)

For Nancy the angels, moons, and stars symbolize her approach. "They remind me to trust the creative forces that I feel have guided me," says Nancy. "When I can do that with something, whether it's a tiny carving or a painting that's taller than I am, the finished piece will always ring true."

One of Nancy's designs—a moon and stars snipped from tin—appears on the following pages. To learn how to make it, simply read on.

A THEME FOR ALL SEASONS

In Nancy Thomas's hands, the moon and stars become a painted tin decoration that's both timely and timeless. At Christmas it glows as a tree topper. During the rest of the year, it rests in a checkerboard stand as a twinkling tabletop accessory.

Materials:
Patterns on page 153
Tracing paper
Permanent felt-tip marker
12" x 18" piece of 26- or 28-gauge tin, brass, copper, or aluminum
Hammer
Drill with ¹⁄₁₆", ⅛", and ¼" bits
Tin snips
Metal file or 80-grit sandpaper
3 (⅛") aluminum pop rivets
Tacky glue
7" length ¼" dowel
2 (18-gauge, ¾"-long) nails with heads
Wire cutters
4"-long x 2"-wide x 1½"-thick wood block
100-grit sandpaper
Paintbrushes
Acrylic paints: green, white, light yellow, gold
Clear satin polyurethane finish
Steel wool
Vinegar

1. Transfer patterns. Using tracing paper and marker, transfer patterns and markings to metal.

2. Drill and cut out designs. At each rivet hole, indent metal with nail; using ⅛" bit, drill. Using tin snips, cut out moon and stars. File edges smooth or sand with 80-grit sandpaper.

3. Attach stars. Referring to photograph for placement, place 1 star on moon, aligning holes. Position rivet and tap with hammer to drive through holes. Turn piece over and hammer rivet flat. Repeat with 2 remaining stars and rivets.

4. Attach dowel. Glue dowel to back of moon where indicated on pattern; let dry. Using ¹⁄₁₆" bit, drill 2 holes where indicated, drilling through dowel and

metal. From back, insert nail through each hole. On front, use wire cutters to cut excess, leaving ⅛" protruding; hammer protrusions flat.

5. Make stand. Using ¼" bit, drill ½"-deep hole in center of wood block. Sand with 100-grit sandpaper. Mark 3 x 3 grid of squares for checkerboard on top. Referring to photograph, paint dowel and top of stand. Let dry. Apply 2 coats polyurethane, letting each coat dry.

6. Paint tin. Soak steel wool in solution of equal parts water and vinegar. Scrub metal. Let dry. Paint moon with 2 or 3 coats of gold, letting each coat dry. In same manner, paint stars light yellow.

7. Display design. For table accessory, insert dowel in hole in stand. For tree topper, remove from stand. Using florist's wire, secure dowel to top of tree.

STAMPED WITH STYLE

Hand-painted holiday greetings are a cinch with these simple stamps. Since you make them from cardboard and twine, you can stamp out dozens of cards on a shoestring.

Materials:
Scraps of corrugated cardboard or matboard
Hot-glue gun and glue sticks
Scraps of twine or thin rope (see Note below)
Disposable plastic plate or tray
Acrylic paints: red, gold, ivory, blue
Paintbrush
Plain purchased notecards and envelopes in assorted sizes

Note: We used ⅛"-diameter twine, but almost any rough-textured twine or thin rope will work; experiment for the best effect.

1. Draw design and make base. Referring to photograph, use a pencil to draw a simple design on cardboard. Trim cardboard slightly larger than design. For handle, stack and glue 2–3 small cardboard squares together. Glue handle on back of cardboard base.

2. Make stamp. Begin at center of design and work outward. Apply a few beads of glue along a small section of traced design. Press twine into glue. Continue gluing twine to cardboard 1 small section at a time until design is completed. Trim excess fibers from twine. Let dry.

3. Paint cards and envelopes with base coat. Pour small amount of desired color paint on plastic plate. Using dampened paper towel, apply paint in overlapping swirls to cover surface completely. Let dry. Repeat if desired.

4. Stamp cards and envelopes. Using paintbrush and contrasting paint, apply paint to twine design on stamp. Then stamp painted card or envelope. Repeat as desired, reapplying paint to twine design as needed. Let dry.

BEAUTIFUL BEADS

Make jewelry and other projects from

tiny mosaics   of modeling clay—it's

easy when you   follow our step-by-step

photographs and   sure-to-succeed

tips. First, learn how to form the beads,

each one a miniature masterpiece.

Then fashion   them into earrings, necklaces,

bracelets, picture frames, or one-of-a-kind buttons. You'll love the results, and your friends will wonder where you've been hiding such a colorful talent. Just turn the page to discover how to turn bright clays into bedazzling beads.

TUBE STRIPES

Gather 2 colors Fimo (1 block each), ruler, razor blade, and toothpick. Necklace on pages 44–45 uses 23 tube stripes. For jewelry-making and other tips, see Bead Basics on page 49.

1. Prepare clay. Roll a log approximately 1" x 1½". Using second color, roll 1 snake approximately ¹⁄₁₆" x 10½". Cut snake into 7 (1½") sections.

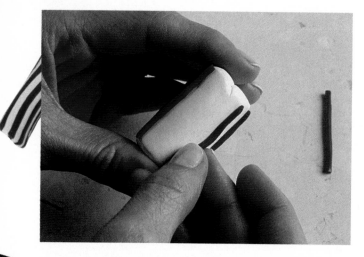

2. Form striped cane. Place 7 snakes around log to form a cane, spacing them evenly.

3. Reduce cane. Gently roll palm of hand over cane, making it thinner and longer, until cane is 12" long.

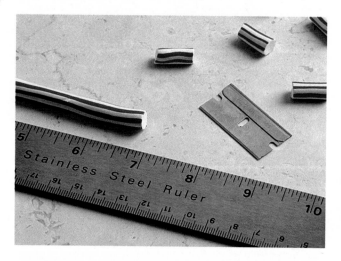

4. Cut cane. Using ruler and razor, measure and cut 24 (½") pieces. Repeat Step 3 and reduce pieces until each is ¾" long.

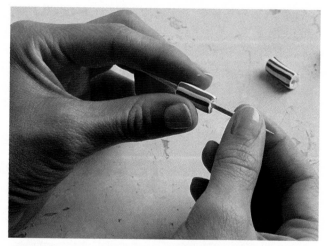

5. Make holes. Gently insert toothpick lengthwise through center of each bead. Bake beads at 275° for 15–20 minutes.

CHECKERBOARDS

Gather 2 colors Fimo (1 block each), brayer, ruler, razor blade, and toothpick. Bracelet on page 45 uses 7 checkerboards and 6 round clay beads. For jewelry-making and other tips, see Bead Basics on page 49.

1. Prepare clay. For each color, roll 8 thin snakes approximately ⅛" x 2".

2. Form a square. Stack snakes in a 4 x 4 square, alternating colors.

3. Roll out sheets. Choose dominant color for beads; using that color, roll 1 (2½" x 3") sheet. Then roll 2 more sheets, each slightly larger than the last. From other color, roll 1 (2½" x 3") sheet. Then roll 1 slightly larger sheet.

4. Wrap log. Beginning with smallest sheet of dominant color and ending with largest, wrap log, alternating colors and trimming excess with razor as you go.

5. Reduce log. Using brayer, gently reduce log until it is approximately ¾" x 9½".

6. Cut log. Using razor and ruler, measure and cut ¼" pieces. For bracelet: From leftover Fimo, roll pea-size beads in desired color.

7. Make holes. Gently insert toothpick through center of each bead. Bake beads at 275° for 15–20 minutes.

MILLEFIORIS

Gather 6 colors of Fimo (1 block each), ruler, razor blade, and toothpick. Pair of earrings on page 45 uses 4 millefioris. For jewelry-making and other instructions, see Bead Basics on page 49.

1. Make jellyroll center. Using 2 colors, roll 1 (1" x 3") sheet from each. Stack sheets as shown and roll to form jellyroll. Reduce by gently rolling palm of hand over jellyroll, making it thinner and longer, until it is approximately ½" x 2".

2. Prepare snakes, sheets, and log for flower petals. Roll a ½" x 2" log from third color, a 2"-square sheet from fourth color, and a 2¼"-square sheet from fifth color. From remaining color, roll a 5"-square sheet and a ¼" x 10" snake. Using razor, cut snake into 5 (2") pieces; press into triangular shapes.

3. Make a petal log. Wrap 2"-square sheet and then 2¼"-square sheet over ½" x 2" log. Gently reduce petal log until it is approximately 10" long. Using razor, cut log into 5 (2") pieces. Press each piece into a teardrop shape.

4. Make flower cane. Place teardrop-shaped petals around jellyroll center. Alternate petal logs and triangular snakes. Roll lightly.

5. Wrap flower cane. Using 5"-square sheet, wrap flower design. Reduce cane until it is approximately ½" in diameter. For earrings: Use leftover clay in desired color to make marble-size beads.

6. Cut cane. Using razor and ruler, measure and cut thin slices from cane. Carefully position slices around solid marble-size beads and press in place.

7. Make holes. Gently insert toothpick through center of each bead. Bake beads at 275° for 15–20 minutes.

Bead Basics

For a source listing for Fimo clay and jewelry findings, see page 156.

• Work on a nonporous surface. Between steps, refrigerate the clay for 5 to 10 minutes to prevent excessive softness. Refrigerate any leftover clay.

• Bake beads in a glass pan. To prevent distortion, thread them on wires and balance the wires on the sides of the pan, suspending the beads.

• To make necklace or bracelet: You will need 24 (8-mm) silver beads for necklace or 14 (4-mm) silver beads for bracelet, nylon-coated wire, 1 silver jump ring, 2 silver crimp beads, 1 silver lobster-claw clasp, and needlenose pliers. Cut wire to desired length, allowing an extra 1½" on each end

for finishing. String beads as shown on pages 44–45, beginning and ending with a silver bead. On each end, thread 1 crimp bead on wire. Thread wire back through crimp bead, leaving a loop of wire at end. Thread wire back through first few beads to secure. Trim excess. Tighten crimp beads with pliers. Attach jump ring to 1 wire loop. Attach clasp to other wire loop.

• To make earrings: You will need 4 (1-mm) and 2 (3-mm) silver beads, 2 silver head pins, 2 silver shepherd-hook wires, and needlenose pliers. Thread beads on head pin as shown on page 45. Using pliers, form loop in remaining length of head pin. Trim excess. Use pliers to attach head pin to shepherd-hook wire.

• For other project ideas, keep reading.

Picture Frame

Christmas Ornament

Bud Vase

Brooch

Flowerpot

Buttons

Fine Finishes

Create a picture frame with beads and an all-metal frame. First, remove the glass and back from the frame and set aside. Cover the frame border with a paper-thin sheet of clay. Reduce the bead cane to the width of the frame border. Cut the cane into thin slices and press them on the clay-covered border. Bake at 275° for 25 minutes. Let cool, and reassemble the frame.

To make a Christmas ornament, string beads to form a star. Simply form a loop in 1 end of a length of heavyweight wire, string your favorite beads in any combination, and then bend the wire. Repeat this process 4 more times; then secure the wire at the top of the star. For a hanger, add a loop of silk cording or narrow ribbon.

Flatter a clay flowerpot with flat beads. After you cut the beads, arrange them around the rim. Bake the pot at 275° for 25 minutes; then paint the base, if desired.

For a bud vase with flair, cover an empty glass bottle with beads in mix-and-match colors. Simply arrange the beads on a bottle as desired, leaving the bottom uncovered. Bake at 275° for 30 minutes.

Create a classic brooch with round beads. To make the pin base, form a circle using a ¼" strip of clay (the circle should be just large enough to hold the desired number of beads). Bake the circle at 275° for 18 minutes. Using silicone glue, glue beads to the circle. Glue a pin back to the clay circle.

Bloomin' buttons! Millefiori means "many flowers," and that's just what you'll be wearing with these buttons. Reduce a bead cane to 1" and then cut ¼" pieces. Using a toothpick, poke 2 holes in the center of each button. Bake at 275° for 15–20 minutes.

51

GIFT BAGS WITH PANACHE

These handmade gift bags, designed by the Oregon-based company Loose Ends, are sturdy yet stylish—the perfect containers for holiday gifts. Natural fiber accents provide pleasing color and added texture.

Materials:
Thin, single-sided corrugated cardboard
Craft knife
Hot-glue gun and glue sticks
Embellishments such as paper braid, paper twine, colored twine, ribbon, twigs, and raffia

Note: For corrugated cardboard and embellishments, see source listing on page 156.

1. Determine desired size of bag. Add desired widths of front, back, and 2 gussets of bag, plus 1" (for glue tab) to determine width to cut. Next, add desired finished height, plus half of gusset width plus ½" (for bottom flap), plus 1½" to determine height to cut.

2. Cut and score corrugated cardboard. Cut corrugated cardboard according to above measurements. Score cardboard along fold lines (indicated by broken lines below) according to measurements. Cut bottom flaps along gusset score lines (Diagram 1).

3. Fold cardboard and glue. Fold top down 1½" to inside along score line and glue. Fold along all side score lines. Glue 1" tab to inside of gusset to complete sides of bag. To close bottom, fold in gusset flaps first and then front and back flaps; glue (Diagram 2).

4. Attach handles and embellish. Referring to photograph for ideas, glue paper braid or paper twine handles to front and back, or punch holes in top of bag and knot colored twine to form handles. Decorate bag with embellishments as desired.

Wrapping Up Loose Ends

We discovered Loose Ends while searching for a mail-order source for out-of-the-ordinary papers and thought you'd like to know about them, too.

Loose Ends began seven years ago in owners Art and Sandi Reinke's garage. Today, Loose Ends employs 12 people and claims clients such as Macy's and Walt Disney.

One look through Loose Ends' catalog and it's obvious why success has been so swift. Their handmade papers, natural-fiber ribbons, papers with Earth-friendly prints, plus ideas for creative wraps and other projects are irresistible, enticing creative hands to get busy. To order the catalog, see the source listing on page 156.

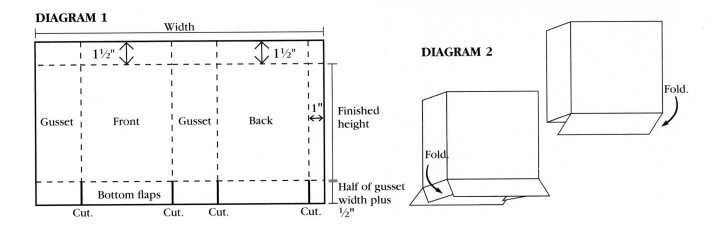

DIAGRAM 1

Width

1½"   1½"

Gusset | Front | Gusset | Back

1" Finished height

Bottom flaps

Cut.   Cut.   Cut.   Cut.

Half of gusset width plus ½"

DIAGRAM 2

Fold.

Fold.

Fold.

Middy-Braid Design

STITCH STOCKINGS WITH A FLOURISH

Adorn these nubby canvas stockings with swirls of soutache or middy braid, and then top them with soft wool cuffs. The contrasting textures and colors make these a pair of stockings Santa's bound to notice.

Materials for 2 stockings:
Patterns on pages 144–47
Tracing paper
Dressmaker's pen
½ yard 60"-wide oatmeal hemp canvas or linen (see Note below)
1 package soutache trim or middy braid
Thread to match fabrics
Fabric glue (optional)
Size 18 sewing-machine needle
⅓ yard white or cream wool
Knitting needle (for turning)
Small amount polyester stuffing (optional)
½ yard lightweight lining fabric

Note: Prewash and press canvas. Stocking patterns do not include ¼" seam allowances. See page 156 for source listings for hemp canvas and trims.

1. Transfer stocking pattern and cut fabric. Using tracing paper and dressmaker's pen, transfer desired stocking pattern to canvas, adding ¼" seam allowances, and cut 2.

2. Transfer design pattern and apply trim. Using tracing paper and dressmaker's pen, transfer desired trim design to stocking front by poking holes at ¼" intervals along design lines to mark canvas. To apply trim, slipstitch or glue trim along pattern lines, tucking ends under.

3. Stitch stocking. (Note: Double-stitched seams are recommended for canvas to prevent raveling.) With right sides facing and raw edges aligned, use size 18 needle to stitch stocking front to stocking back, leaving top open. Clip curves and turn. Press.

4. Make cuff and hanger. For cuff, cut a 10" x 12¾" rectangle from wool. With right sides facing, fold rectangle in half widthwise. Stitch 10" ends together; turn. With wrong sides facing, fold in half lengthwise. If desired, lightly pad cuff with polyester stuffing. Insert stocking top inside cuff, aligning raw edges at top. Machine-stitch cuff to stocking.

For hanger, cut a 2½" x 6" strip from canvas. With wrong sides facing, fold strip in half lengthwise. Stitch along long edge and across 1 end. Using knitting needle, turn; fold in half and stitch ends together to form loop. Pin loop to stocking back, 1" from right side seam. Baste.

5. Make and attach lining. Using tracing paper and dressmaker's pen, trace and cut out 2 stocking pieces for lining, adding ¼" seam allowance. Stitch pieces together, leaving top edge open and 4" opening in side seam above heel. Clip curves but do not turn. With right sides facing, slip lining over stocking, matching side seams and top edges. Stitch lining to stocking around top edge, catching ends of hanger in seam. Turn stocking through opening in lining. Slipstitch opening closed. Tuck lining inside stocking. Turn down cuff.

A Fabled Fabric

Leslie Batchelor, a designer in Olympia, Washington, uses hemp textiles imported from Hungary to create everything from the embellished stockings shown here to pillows and upholstered furniture.

Perhaps the oldest fiber worked by human hands, hemp is more durable than cotton or linen. Colonists used it to make sails for ships, and Thomas Jefferson wrote the first draft of the Declaration of Independence on paper made from hemp.

Today, hemp is often blended with cotton and silk to achieve a range of textures. You can order hemp fabrics through Leslie's shop, Hands All Around; for information, see page 156.

Soutache Design

IDEAS
USE YOUR MARBLES

Dust off those old marbles — be they frosties, clearies, swirlies, or steelies — and put them back in the game. These projects are so easy, you'll think they're child's play.

Ring Around a Trivet

Gather 4"-, 6"-, or 8"-square white ceramic tiles. Using clear silicone glue, glue 1 marble to each bottom corner. Let dry.

Marble-ous Ornaments

From 24-gauge wire, cut 6 (18") lengths. Holding lengths together as 1, bend wire in half to make a U-shape. Nestle a marble in bottom of U. Wrap wire around marble, spacing lengths evenly and twisting them together at top. Repeat wrapping and twisting to add more marbles. At top, twist wire to make a hanger loop, cutting off excess.

Lighten a Lamp

Using clear silicone glue, glue marbles to base of a plain glass hurricane lamp. Set marbles in rows or in a random pattern—or do both, as we did here. Look for hurricane lamps at hardware stores or discount centers.

Ring Napkins with Flair

For each napkin ring: Using clear silicone glue, glue 6 jumbo marbles together in a circle. Let dry. Wrap marbles with 2 (36") lengths of 20-gauge galvanized wire, using needlenose pliers to tuck in ends.

Instructions for checkerboard begin on page 61.

TREASURED TRADITIONS

Get in the game and create an old-fashioned holiday. Make your first move with this antiqued checkerboard, then follow up with other winning projects and recipes. You'll score points for your creativity, but your greatest reward will be the fun you had in the process.

AN OLD-FASHIONED CHECKERBOARD— FROM SQUARE ONE

**It's easy to recapture yesteryear's playworn effects.
In seven simple steps, here's how.**

Materials:
14½" square ¾"-thick pine or birch plywood
30" length of ¾" x ⅝" molding
Saw
Wood glue
6 fourpenny nails
Foam brushes: 1 (2") and 2 (1")
Hide glue
Acrylic paints: green, red, off-white, black
100-grit sandpaper
Oil stains: light honey (such as pine), ebony or
  dark brown (such as walnut)
Old toothbrush
Satin oil-based or lacquer spray finish
24 unfinished wood playing pieces

1. Prepare board. Cut 2 (14½"-long) pieces of molding; attach to opposite sides of wood square with glue and nails. Using pencil and ruler, mark 12" square in center of board; mark square into an 8 x 8 grid of 64 (1½") squares. Using 2" brush, randomly apply thin layer of hide glue to partially cover surface. Let dry.

2. Paint board. Using 1" brush, paint border green; let dry. Paint squares, alternating red and off-white as shown; let dry. As paint dries, a crackle effect will appear in areas covered with hide glue.

3. Sand board. To create aged appearance, sand edges of board and parts of painted surface. Sand some areas lightly and some heavily to simulate uneven wear. Using damp rag, wipe board clean.

4. Apply light stain. Using remaining 1" brush, apply light stain, covering painted surface, edges, and unfinished back of board. Using dry rag, wipe off excess. Let dry.

5. Apply dark stain. To simulate grime accumulated through years of use, wipe on dark stain with dry rag, applying stain unevenly and wiping off excess. Let dry.

6. Spatter-paint surface. Dip bristles of dry toothbrush in black paint; shake off excess. Drawing index finger across bristles, lightly and unevenly spatter surface. Let dry.

7. Apply finish. To protect surface, apply 2 coats of spray finish, letting each coat dry completely. To antique unfinished playing pieces, repeat steps 2–7, painting 12 pieces off-white and 12 pieces red.

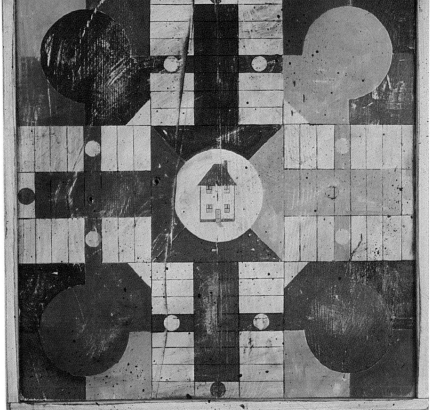

Child's Parcheesi

Fair Games

For Mary Thompson of Pinedale, Wyoming, antique game boards have two great virtues: graphic beauty and nostalgic appeal.

Mary started collecting old game boards in the 1980s. "I loved their colors and patterns, which reminded me of old quilts," she remembers.

Mary wasn't the only one taking notice; collectors were, too. Twenty-five years ago, a game board might have sold for a couple of dollars; today, that same board could fetch more than $1,000.

As prices rose, Mary began crafting replicas. It proved a happy match for her woodworking skills and her training in art history and education. Eventually, her pastime grew into a business—named, appropriately, Games People Played.

Good Moves

Mary sells most of her game boards through her mail-order business. (Two of them are pictured here; for these and others, see the source listing on page 156.) But when we asked her to design a checkerboard for readers of *American Country Christmas*, she happily agreed.

Mary also offered a few suggestions for making a game board:

• **Plan your strategy.** Perform each step on several boards at once, and you'll have some to give away and one to keep.

• **Gather your gear.** Materials for the game board, including hide glue, can be found at a lumberyard or hardware store. Unfinished wood playing pieces are carried by many craft stores. Alternatively, you can order an unfinished board (with molding already attached) and playing pieces from Games People Played; for a source listing, see page 156.

• **Change the rules.** To make the project simpler, start with a breadboard or pine plywood board measuring 14" x 16", omitting the molding altogether.

• **Play it safe.** Cover your work surface with newsprint or a dropcloth, and wear rubber gloves to protect your hands.

When applying spray finish, always work in a well-ventilated area. Place the project in a large box and spray into the box to contain the spray.

Chinese Checkers

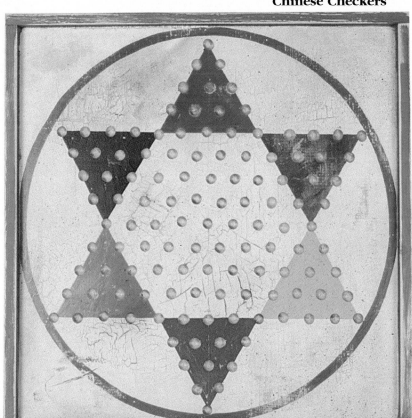

NATURE'S DESIGNS

Imprint handkerchiefs and other linens with images of real leaves. With this technique, knocking out beautiful botanicals is a breeze.

Materials:
Fabric to be imprinted (see Note below)
White vinegar
Freezer paper: 2 (12") squares, 1 (4") square
Various fern fronds or other leaves
Hammer
Black fine-tip permanent fabric marker

Note: Sources for white 45-count linen and ready-made white linen handkerchiefs are on page 156.

1. Prepare materials. Wash, dry, and press fabric. Pour vinegar in 1 bowl and water in another bowl. On flat surface, layer 1 (12") square of freezer paper (waxed side down), fabric (right side up), frond, and remaining 12" square of freezer paper (waxed side up).

2. Make and set imprint. Using flat side of hammerhead, gently tap hammer over frond. Remove fabric and soak in vinegar for 1 minute. Rinse in water. Roll in towel to remove excess water; iron dry.

3. Label imprint. With waxed side down, iron 4" square of freezer paper to wrong side of imprint to stabilize fabric as you write. With marker, write name on right side. Iron over name; remove freezer paper.

Make a Good Impression

Follow these tips for making perfect imprints.
- **Get testy.** Experiment on muslin first.
- **For everything there is a season.** Leaves picked in spring or summer yield bright green prints; leaves picked in autumn make lighter prints.
- **Heat waves.** When ironing the design, use moderate heat and iron over the imprint only once or twice.

TWICE AS NICE

These delicious gifts score on two counts. Each can be enjoyed as is,
straight from the jar, plus it's the star ingredient in a companion recipe.
Write the recipe on the back of your gift tag to present a treat
that's even tastier the second time around.

Date-Orange Chutney

2 oranges
4 cups sugar
5½ cups cider vinegar (5% acidity)
1½ teaspoons dried crushed red pepper
1 pound pitted dates, chopped
2 medium onions, chopped
2½ cups raisins

Grate rind from oranges; set rind aside. Peel and discard pith from oranges; chop orange sections, discarding seeds.

Combine sugar, vinegar, and crushed red pepper in a large Dutch oven. Cook over low heat, stirring constantly, until sugar dissolves. Add chopped orange, dates, onion, raisins, and half of grated orange rind to Dutch oven. Bring to a boil; reduce heat, and simmer, uncovered, for 2 hours or until mixture is very thick, stirring occasionally. Remove from heat, and stir in the remaining orange rind.

Spoon hot chutney into hot jars, filling to ½ inch from top. Remove air bubbles; wipe jar rims. Cover at once with metal lids, and screw on bands. Process in boiling-water bath 10 minutes. Let chutney stand at room temperature at least 2 weeks before serving. Refrigerate after opening. Yield: 7 half-pints.

Chutney-Glazed Pork Chops

1 (6-ounce) package long-grain-and-
    wild rice mix
½ cup sliced celery
1 tablespoon butter or margarine, melted
⅓ cup chopped pecans, toasted
½ cup Date-Orange Chutney (see recipe)
3 tablespoons orange juice
4 (¾-inch-thick) bone-in pork chops
½ teaspoon salt
¼ teaspoon pepper
2 tablespoons vegetable oil

Prepare rice mix according to package directions; set aside.

Cook celery in butter in a small skillet over medium-high heat, stirring constantly, until tender. Add celery and pecans to rice; stir well.

Combine Date-Orange Chutney and orange juice in a small saucepan; cook over medium-low heat, stirring constantly, until chutney melts. Stir ¼ cup chutney mixture into rice mixture; spoon rice mixture into a lightly greased 8-inch-square baking dish.

Sprinkle chops evenly with salt and pepper; brown chops on both sides in hot oil. Arrange chops over rice mixture; spoon remaining chutney mixture over chops. Cover and bake at 350° for 40 minutes or until chops are tender. Yield: 4 servings.

The Case for Canning

Canning gives these pantry presents the longest shelf life. Though the process might seem intimidating at first, these steps make it safe and simple.

• **The essentials.** The directions in these recipes are for using traditional canning jars and lids. If you use the newer, decorative jars shown at left, follow the manufacturer's instructions.

For processing traditional jars, a water-bath canner with rack is ideal. But for processing just a few jars at a time, substitute a stock pot or Dutch oven several inches deeper than the jars. If you don't have a rack that will fit in the bottom of your pot, substitute a folded kitchen towel.

You'll also need a timer, a narrow rubber spatula, and standard jars with metal bands and lids. The lids must be new since the sealing compound works only once; follow the manufacturer's instructions for heating them before use.

• **A clean record.** Wash the jars in warm, soapy water, rinse them well, and keep them hot (a dishwasher works well for this). If processing time is under 10 minutes, sterilize the jars first by boiling them in water for 10 minutes.

• **Filling the bill.** When filling the jars, follow recipe directions for leaving headspace. Run a spatula around the inside of the jars to remove air bubbles. Wipe the rims clean, put on the lids, and screw on the bands, tightening them to fit snugly.

• **Boiling points.** Because these recipes call for packing hot mixtures into hot jars, you can place the filled jars directly into the boiling-water bath. Water should flow around the jars, leveling 1 to 2 inches above the lids. When the water returns to a boil, cover the canner or pot and set your timer for the processing time.

• **The deal on seals.** After the jars cool 12 to 24 hours, make sure they've sealed properly. Each lid should be concave, with a downward curve you can feel. (Refrigerate jars with faulty seals and use them right away.) Remove the metal bands and store the jars in a cool, dark, dry place.

Chunky Spiced-Apple Muffins

Spiced Apples

**5 pounds medium cooking apples
  (about 10 apples)
1 gallon water
3/4 cup lemon juice
2 (3-inch) sticks cinnamon
1 tablespoon whole cloves
1 teaspoon whole allspice
4 cups sugar
3 1/2 cups water
1/2 cup cider vinegar (5% acidity)
1/4 cup red cinnamon candies**

  Peel and core apples; cut into quarters. Combine apple quarters, 1 gallon water, and lemon juice in a large bowl; set aside. Place cinnamon sticks, cloves, and allspice on a square of cheesecloth; tie with string. Combine spice bag, sugar, and remaining ingredients in a large Dutch oven. Bring to a boil; boil 5 minutes. Remove from heat.
  Drain apple quarters in a colander, and add to syrup mixture in Dutch oven; let stand 10 minutes. Return Dutch oven to heat. Bring to a boil; reduce heat, and simmer, uncovered, 10 minutes, stirring occasionally. Remove from heat, and cool slightly.
  Drain apples, reserving syrup in Dutch oven; bring syrup to a boil. Pack hot apples into hot jars, filling to 1/2 inch from top. Cover apples with boiling syrup, filling to 1/2 inch from top. Remove air bubbles; wipe jar rims. Cover with metal lids, and screw on bands. Process in boiling-water bath 20 minutes for quarts and pints. Yield: 2 quarts or 4 pints.

Chunky Spiced-Apple Muffins

**2 cups all-purpose flour
1 tablespoon baking powder
1/4 teaspoon salt
1/4 cup sugar
1 teaspoon ground cinnamon
1 large egg, lightly beaten
1/2 cup milk
1/4 cup molasses
1/4 cup vegetable oil
1 cup finely chopped Spiced Apples
  (see recipe)**

  Combine first 5 ingredients in a large bowl; make a well in center of mixture. Combine egg and next 3 ingredients; add to dry ingredients, stirring until just moistened. Fold in Spiced Apples.
  Spoon batter into greased muffin pans, filling three-fourths full. Bake at 400° for 16 minutes or until golden. Remove from pans immediately. Yield: 9 muffins.

Pumpkin Butter

1 (29-ounce) can pumpkin
1½ cups sugar
¾ cup apple juice
2 teaspoons ground cinnamon
2 teaspoons ground ginger
1 teaspoon ground nutmeg
½ teaspoon ground cloves

Combine all ingredients in a large saucepan; stir well.

Bring pumpkin mixture to a boil; reduce heat, and simmer 30 minutes or until thickened, stirring frequently.

Spoon hot pumpkin mixture into hot jars, filling to ¼ inch from top. Remove air bubbles; wipe jar rims.

Cover at once with metal lids, and screw on bands. Process in boiling-water bath 10 minutes. Yield: 5 half-pints.

Pumpkin-Pecan Cheesecake

½ cup chopped pecans
¼ cup firmly packed brown sugar
2 tablespoons butter or margarine, softened
1 (8-ounce) package cream cheese, softened
1 (3-ounce) package cream cheese, softened
⅓ cup firmly packed brown sugar
2 large eggs
¾ cup Pumpkin Butter (see recipe)
1 (9-inch) graham cracker crust

Combine pecans and ¼ cup brown sugar; cut in butter with a pastry blender until mixture is crumbly. Set aside.

Beat cream cheese at high speed of an electric mixer until smooth. Add ⅓ cup brown sugar; beat well. Add eggs, one at a time, beating after each addition. Stir in Pumpkin Butter. Pour mixture into crust. Bake at 350° for 40 minutes. Sprinkle pecan mixture over pie, and bake 5 additional minutes or until butter and sugar melt. Cool on a wire rack; cover and chill at least 4 hours. Yield: one 9-inch cheesecake.

Give Tags Your Own Stamp

The gift foods pictured on pages 66 and 102 owe much of their charm to their packaging: interesting containers, glittery sheer ribbons, and handmade gift tags.

The tags are simple to make when you use rubber stamps. Because they are increasingly popular among crafters, stamps are easy to find. Look for them—as well as stamp pads, handmade papers, and writing pens—in craft stores and stationery shops.

While you're shopping for stamps, you may want to pick up sealing wax and wax stamps. Glossy medallions of stamped sealing wax punctuate a tag with panache. For source listings for handmade papers, ribbons, sealing wax, and the stamps you see here, see page 156.

NATIVE TALENT

When it comes to decorating, Deby Harvey of Olympia, Washington, relaxes and takes her cues from nature.

A branch. A flower. A patch of wild grass going to seed. As commonplace as they may seem, they're Deby's inspirations. When she creates her holiday decorations, she takes her direction from the freeform beauty of natural materials.

"I never try to force materials into an arrangement," she says. "Instead, I let their natural shapes guide the foundation of my designs."

Deby's house is nestled in the foothills of Washington's Cascade Mountains. It's surrounded by fields and woods that yield the raw materials she uses both at home and in her business, Overleaf Designs. She gleans grapevines, ivy, and dogwood branches from the yard; wildflowers and grasses are plucked from nearby fields. "Whatever catches my eye, whatever the season offers—that's what I'll use."

Deby claims that working with greenery and other natural materials is easier than it looks and that anyone can do it. Here are some of her ideas on making arrangements with natural appeal.

Deby's Top 10 Tips

1. Choose materials that appeal to you, regardless of trends.

2. Look in your own back yard for branches and greenery. Even the humblest plants can look great in an effective arrangement.

3. Large-scale arrangements will seem less intimidating if you try them on a small scale first. You can play with the smaller version, ensuring that the large design will suit you.

4. String berries, dried fruit, and other heavy items on dental floss, which provides a strong base. One of Deby's favorite garlands combines fresh cranberries and dried rose hips.

5. When working with ivy, choose a variety with short-stemmed leaves to create fullness.

6. Spray-paint naturals to keep them fresh longer and add a bit of glitter. Be sure your naturals are completely dry before you spray-paint them.

7. Both potted trees and small cut ones make fine tabletop Christmas trees. Just be sure to anchor the cut trees securely in their bases so they won't topple over.

8. Deby uses gold spray paint and patina to give terra-cotta pots a bronze finish like the one shown on page 73. To order the patina she uses, see the source listing on page 157.

9. "Once you get an idea, let it take shape," Deby advises. "By using your intuition when creating a design, you allow your own style to shine through."

10. For inspiration, begin with the ideas that follow. On the next three pages, Deby shows you three different ways to trim a tree for the table.

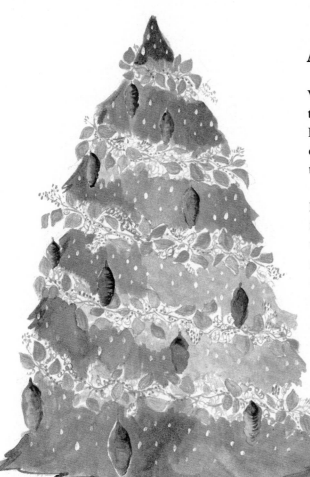

A Tree to Pine For

When Deby brainstormed the ideas for the tabletop trees shown on this page, she asked her friend Becky Havekost, owner of Sunny Brook Murals, to depict her designs in watercolors. The illustration at left shows a tree inspired by winter woodlands.

To re-create it, string your tree with tiny white lights. For the main garland, wrap long, thin pieces of Spanish moss around lengths of seeded eucalyptus, using florist's wire where necessary to stabilize the garland. For smaller garlands, string cranberries on dental floss. Wind the cranberry garlands around the main garland and around the tree. Top pinecones with hanger loops of gold wire or florist's wire, and hang the cones as ornaments.

All That Glitters

Deby used a simple color scheme and a spare touch with decorations to give the tree at right classic appeal.

First, string your tree with lots of tiny white lights. For the main garland, buy or make a boxwood garland and loosely wrap it with lengths of gold angel hair. Wind the garland around the tree.

For a second garland, dust lengths of ivy with gold spray-paint. Wind the ivy garland around the tree in a different direction from the first garland.

If desired, add ornaments of your own choosing. Deby leaves the tree as is, preferring the simplicity of gleaming garlands and twinkling white lights.

A TREE IN A TWINKLING

A tabletop tree—like this one by Deby Harvey—packs visual punch with
a minimal investment of time and materials. The garland and
twiggy stars assemble easily for a holiday decoration that's a natural.

A Glittery Greenery Garland

1. Wind 1 length of ivy around another. Add a third by tucking 1 end between twist of first 2 to secure. Continue adding ivy until garland is desired length.

2. To stabilize garland, anchor ends of ivy lengths with short lengths of 26-gauge florist's wire. Working on a covered surface, spray-paint garland gold. Let dry.

3. To attach sprigs of rose hip to garland, twist short lengths of florist wire around stem of each sprig and wire stem to garland. Wind garland around tree.

Little Twiggy Stars

  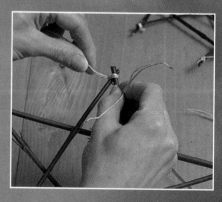

1. For each ornament, arrange 5 (4"-long) twigs into a star shape. (For a large star like the tree topper shown at right, use 8"-long twigs.)

2. Using a hot-glue gun and glue sticks, carefully glue ends of twigs together to secure points of star. Let dry.

3. Wrap a short length of raffia around each point, knotting ends to secure. For hanger, tie a loop of raffia around 1 point.

ON THE BUTTON

Odds and ends from the button box whirl around a snowy tree skirt and matching ornaments. Cut out the batting, attach the buttons, and stitch and pink the edges—who would have dreamed something so festive could be so easy?

Tree Skirt

Materials:
3 yards 54"-wide unbleached needled-cotton
  batting (see Note below)
1 (36") piece of string
Pushpin
Dressmaker's pen
Assorted colors embroidery floss
Assorted buttons (see Note below)
Pinking shears

    Note: *For source listings for needled-cotton batting and buttons by the pound, see page 157.*

    1. Cut out skirt top and backing. From batting, cut 2 (54") squares. For skirt top, fold 1 square in half and then in fourths to find center. Unfold square. To make a compass, tie dressmaker's pen to 1 end of string; measure 27" of string and tie pushpin to other end. Referring to Diagram, stick pushpin in center of batting and draw a 54"-diameter circle. Measure 5" of string and draw a 10"-diameter circle in center of 54" circle. Cut out outer circle. Cut a straight line from outer edge to inner circle; cut out inner circle.

    Using skirt top as a pattern, cut skirt backing from remaining batting square.

    2. Attach buttons. Referring to photograph for placement, stitch buttons to skirt top, using 3 strands of floss and leaving a 1½" margin around all edges.

    3. Stitch top and backing together. Aligning raw edges, stack skirt top (right side up) on top of backing; pin to secure layers. Using 3 strands of floss, stitch layers together with a running stitch 1" from all edges.

    4. Trim edges. Using pinking shears, trim all edges ½" from stitching line.

DIAGRAM

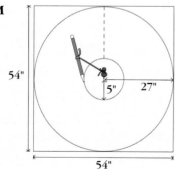

Tree Ornament

Materials:
Pattern on page 141
Tracing paper
Dressmaker's pen
Scrap of unbleached needled-cotton batting
  (see Note below)
Assorted colors embroidery floss
Assorted buttons (see Note below)
Pinking shears

    Note: *For source listings for needled-cotton batting and buttons by the pound, see page 157.*

    1. Cut out ornament. Use tracing paper and dressmaker's pen to transfer pattern to batting; cut 2.

    2. Attach buttons. Using 3 strands of floss and referring to photograph for placement, attach buttons.

    3. Stitch front and back together. Aligning raw edges, stack front (right side up) on top of back; pin layers to secure. Using 3 strands of floss, stitch layers together with a running stitch 1" from all edges.

    4. Trim edges. Using pinking shears, trim all edges ½" from stitching line.

    5. Make hanger. Using 3 strands of floss, stitch loop through top of ornament and knot to secure.

Snowman Ornament

Materials:
Patterns on page 141
Tracing paper
Dressmaker's pen
Scrap of unbleached needled-cotton batting
  (see Note below)
Scrap of black felt
Pinking shears
Embroidery floss: black, assorted colors
Assorted buttons (see Note below)

    Note: *For source listing for needled-cotton batting and buttons by the pound, see page 157.*

    1. Cut out ornament. Use tracing paper and dressmaker's pen to transfer pattern to batting; cut 2.

Transfer hat pattern to felt and cut 1 with pinking shears; set aside.

2. Attach buttons. Using 3 strands of floss and referring to photograph for placement, attach buttons. Using 3 strands of black floss and running stitch, stitch mouth; using French knots, stitch eyes. (See page 131 for Embroidery Diagrams.)

3. Stitch pieces together. Aligning raw edges, stack front (right side up) on top of back; pin layers to secure. Using 3 strands of floss, stitch layers together with a running stitch 1" from all edges.

4. Trim edges. Using pinking shears, trim all edges ½" from stitching line.

5. Make hat. Using 2 strands of black floss, run a gathering stitch ¼" from edge of black felt circle. Pull thread to gather circle into shape of brimmed hat; knot to secure. Tack hat to snowman's head.

6. Make hanger. Using 3 strands of black floss, stitch loop through top of ornament and knot to secure.

MONKEY BUSINESS

Do you recall those monkey dolls sewn from red-heeled work socks?
For generations children have loved the fuzz off these saucy stuffed animals.
Our monkeys, crafted from socks in today's colors, are every
bit as impish as the ones you remember.

Girl Monkey Doll

Materials:
Patterns on pages 148–49
1 adult-size pair red ragg socks with contrasting
    heel and toe
Dressmaker's pen
Thread to match socks
1 bag polyester stuffing
Tracing paper
Embroidery floss: 1 skein each black, berry red
$\frac{1}{2}$" buttons: 2 black, 1 berry red
Felt: 2 (9" x 12") pieces berry red, 1 (9" x 12")
    piece gold
$1\frac{1}{4}$"-diameter gold pom-pom
Pinking shears
Fabric glue

Note: See sources listed on page 157 for ragg socks,
wool felt, and kits for traditional red-heeled sock monkeys. Patterns include $\frac{1}{4}$" seam allowances.

1. Make legs and torso. Turn 1 sock inside out.
Use dressmaker's pen to mark center line (Diagram 1).
Stitch $\frac{1}{4}$" from center line and from edge as shown,
leaving crotch open. Cut along center line. Turn right
side out through opening. Firmly stuff legs and torso.
Slipstitch closed. Handstitch across tops of legs
through all layers, pulling thread tightly.

2. Make arms. Turn remaining sock inside out. Use
dressmaker's pen to mark center line (Diagram 2).
Stitch $\frac{1}{4}$" from center line and from edge as shown.
Cut across arm section at top of center line and along
center line to separate arms (Diagram 3). Turn arms
right side out. Stuff loosely. Gather each opening and
secure thread; slipstitch arms securely to torso (see
photograph for placement).

DIAGRAM 1

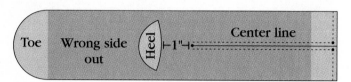

DIAGRAM 2

DIAGRAM 3

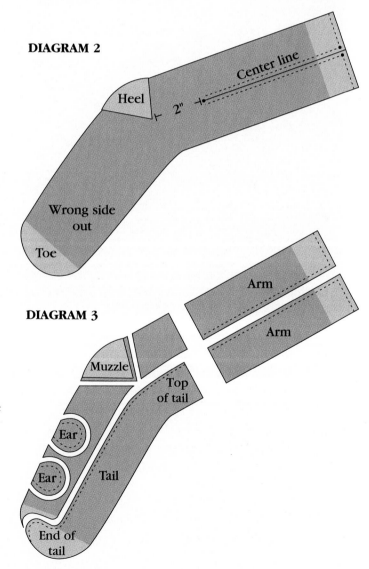

Girl Monkey Doll

7. Add facial features. For mouth, transfer pattern onto muzzle. Using 6 strands of floss, stemstitch mouth red and make black French knots for nostrils. (For Embroidery Diagrams, see page 131.)

For eyes, sew black buttons to head ¾" apart just above muzzle. Using 6 strands of black floss, longstitch eyelashes above eyes (see photograph).

8. Make hat. Using tracing paper, transfer hat pattern to 1 piece of berry red felt and cut out. Stitch pieces together along straight sides to form cone. Trim excess fabric from seam allowance at tip of hat to reduce bulk. Turn. Stitch gold pom-pom to top of hat.

9. Make pinafore. Using tracing paper, transfer pinafore pattern to gold felt and cut out. Transfer pinafore pattern to remaining piece of berry red felt. Using pinking shears, cut out pinafore, adding ¼" all around. Center and glue gold pinafore on top of berry red pinafore; let dry.

Cut 2 (⅝" x 4½") waistband strips from berry red felt. Stitch 1 end of each strip to wrong side of

3. Make muzzle. Cut off heel from remainder of sock, adding ¼" seam allowance (Diagram 3). Turn edges under and baste top edge and two-thirds of bottom edge to front of torso, 1" below toe. Stuff firmly; slipstitch closed.

4. Make tail. Cut tail from remainder of sock as shown in Diagram 3. Stitch, leaving top of tail open; turn. Stuff firmly; gather opening and secure thread. Slipstitch tail to back of monkey, with top of tail even with top of white section.

5. Make ears. Using tracing paper, transfer ear pattern to remainder of folded sock, aligning straight edge with fold, and cut 2. Cut ears apart along straight edge to make 4 ears. For each ear, stitch 2 ear pieces together, leaving straight edge open; turn. Turn edges under and slipstitch closed; make a tuck in center of ear front and tack. Stitch to head, aligning bottom of ear with corner of muzzle.

6. Make neck. Gather body just above arms. Pull thread to shape neck; secure thread.

Boy Monkey Doll

80

pinafore (see pattern). Place pinafore on doll to check fit. Overlap ends of waistband on back and pin. Tuck ends of straps under waistband in back and pin. Remove pinafore. Stitch ends of straps to waistband. Cut buttonhole in 1 end of waistband. Sew button to other end. Transfer pattern and cut out 1 heart from berry red felt; glue to center front of pinafore.

Boy Monkey Doll

Materials:
Patterns on pages 148–49
1 adult-size pair green ragg socks with contrasting heel and toe
Dressmaker's pen
Thread to match socks
1 bag polyester stuffing
Tracing paper
Embroidery floss: 1 skein each black, berry red
Buttons: 1 (³⁄₄") gold, 2 (⁵⁄₈") black
Felt: 2 (9" x 12") pieces forest green, 1 (9" x 12") piece berry red
1¹⁄₄"-diameter berry red pom-pom
Pinking shears
Fabric glue

Note: See sources listed on page 157 for ragg socks, wool felt, and kits for traditional red-heeled sock monkeys. Patterns include ¼" seam allowances.

1. Make doll. Repeat steps 1–7 for girl doll, except use boy's mouth pattern, omit eyelashes, and do not gather to shape neck.

2. Make hat. Repeat Step 8 for girl doll, using forest green felt for hat and berry red pom-pom.

3. Make jacket. Using tracing paper, transfer jacket pattern to berry red felt and cut out. Repeat to cut jacket collar from forest green felt. Pink top and front edge of collar (see pattern). Glue to inside of jacket, with pinked edges ¼" from edge of jacket. Cut arm slits and buttonhole on left front of jacket (see pattern). Put jacket on doll. Mark button placement on right front of jacket; sew on gold button.

The Sock Exchange

Ann Mooney of Jamondas Press in Ann Arbor, Michigan, is an encyclopedia of information about sock monkeys. She has also sewn many a doll from socks. Some years ago, after she had taken hundreds of photographs of her son posing with her creations, Ann's friends urged her to "do something" with the pictures. She already had an interest in writing, and she put it to work authoring fanciful picture books about the dolls.

Ann says that red-heeled socks—the traditional choice for old-fashioned sock monkeys—date to at least the 1880s, when Nelson Knitting Mills in Rockford, Illinois, began churning out the socks on their flatbed machines. To some people the quirky, slightly irregular red heels looked like smiles. But it wasn't until the 1940s that people began translating the smile into the whole monkey. The monkeys became so popular that Nelson Knitting Mills started selling patterns and instructions with each pair of red-heeled socks.

Ann says monkey dolls were most popular in the 1950s and 1960s, after which their fortunes waned. But the mid-1980s brought rediscovery, and now some collectors can't get enough of the mischievous creatures.

"There's really a new interest in sock monkeys," Ann claims, and it may have something to do with nostalgia. "Sock monkeys seem to evoke more detailed memories than most toys," Ann says. "People remember their monkey's name, who made the doll or gave it to them, what games they used to play with it. I've been surprised by the number of people who still have their monkeys, long after their sandbox days are over."

For information about Jamondas Press and the traditional red-heeled socks, see page 157.

IDEAS
MERRY MITTENS

Decorate pairs of purchased mittens for quick gifts. These four styles cover every fashion contingency—hands down.

Cute As a Button

Gather a variety of colorful novelty buttons. Sew on shank buttons. To attach a two-hole button with $\frac{1}{16}$"- or $\frac{1}{8}$"-wide ribbon, thread the ribbon through a large-eyed needle and stitch through the button and mitten back, leaving ribbon tails on top. Remove the needle, knot the ribbon tails, and trim the ends.

Backhand Brads

Purchase several styles of brads. Arrange them on a mitten back to find a placement you like. Then, following the manufacturer's instructions, attach the brads, adding a drop of fabric glue under each one.

Off the Cuff

The trick to this bracelet of buttons is its foundation: a circlet of wide-link chain fashioned from an old necklace. Measure the circumference of each mitten's cuff. Using wire cutters, cut two lengths of chain to this measurement. Using pliers, pry open the link at one end of each length and reattach it to the other end to form a bracelet. Whipstitch one bracelet to each mitten cuff. Sew an assortment of buttons to the bracelet links, occasionally passing the needle through the cuff for extra stability.

Jingle All the Way

Multicolored bells and ribbon bows make these mittens ring with good cheer. First, tie a bow to the shank of each bell. Then tack the bells to the mitten backs, stitching through the shank and the bow on each.

Mittens by Mail

If you're making multiples of these merry mittens, you can save time by ordering them by mail. For a source listing, see page 157.

Recipe for Cinnamon-Spiced Cider is on page 91.

COUNTRY CHRISTMAS PANTRY

Warm hearts with mugs of steaming cider flavored with cinnamony red-hot candies— just the thing for making spirits bright. Then try some other happy holiday specials, with best wishes from our kitchen to yours.

VISIONS OF SUGARPLUMS

Red-hots, chocolate, peppermint candy, *more* chocolate—
who can resist the candies of Christmas? Play up the season's celebration of
sugar and spice with this sampler of treats made with holiday sweets.

Peppermint Fudge

Vegetable cooking spray
2½ cups sugar
½ cup butter or margarine
1 (5-ounce) can evaporated milk
1 (12-ounce) package semisweet
chocolate morsels (2 cups)
1 (7-ounce) jar marshmallow cream
¾ cup finely crushed hard peppermint
candy
1 teaspoon vanilla extract
Additional crushed hard peppermint candy

Line a greased 9-inch square pan with aluminum foil, allowing foil to extend over edges. Coat foil with cooking spray.

Combine sugar, butter, and milk in a medium saucepan. Bring to a boil over medium heat; boil 5 minutes, stirring constantly. Remove from heat; add chocolate morsels and marshmallow cream, stirring until smooth. Stir in ¾ cup crushed peppermint and vanilla.

Spread mixture into prepared pan; sprinkle with additional crushed peppermint. Cool in pan. To serve, remove fudge from pan, using edges of foil to lift out. Cut fudge into squares; remove foil. Yield: 3 pounds.

Peanut Butter Cookies
with Chocolate Kisses

Peppermint Fudge

Peanut Butter Cookies with Chocolate Kisses

½ cup shortening
½ cup creamy peanut butter
½ cup sugar
½ cup firmly packed brown sugar
1 large egg
2 tablespoons milk
1 teaspoon vanilla extract
1¾ cups all-purpose flour
1 teaspoon baking soda
½ teaspoon salt
½ cup ground unsalted peanuts
2½ tablespoons light corn syrup
2 tablespoons creamy peanut
   butter
38 milk chocolate kisses

Beat shortening and ½ cup peanut butter at medium speed of an electric mixer until smooth; gradually add sugars, beating well.

Add egg, milk, and vanilla; beat well.

Combine flour, soda, and salt; add to shortening mixture, beating well. Cover and chill 30 minutes.

Combine peanuts, corn syrup, and 2 tablespoons peanut butter in a small saucepan. Cook over medium-low heat, stirring constantly, until peanut butter melts.

Shape dough into 1-inch balls; place 2 inches apart on ungreased cookie sheets. Press thumb into each ball of dough, leaving an indentation; fill each indentation with ½ teaspoon peanut mixture.

Bake at 375° for 10 minutes or until lightly browned. Remove from oven; press a chocolate kiss into center of each cookie.

Cool slightly on cookie sheets; remove to wire racks, and cool completely. Yield: 38 cookies.

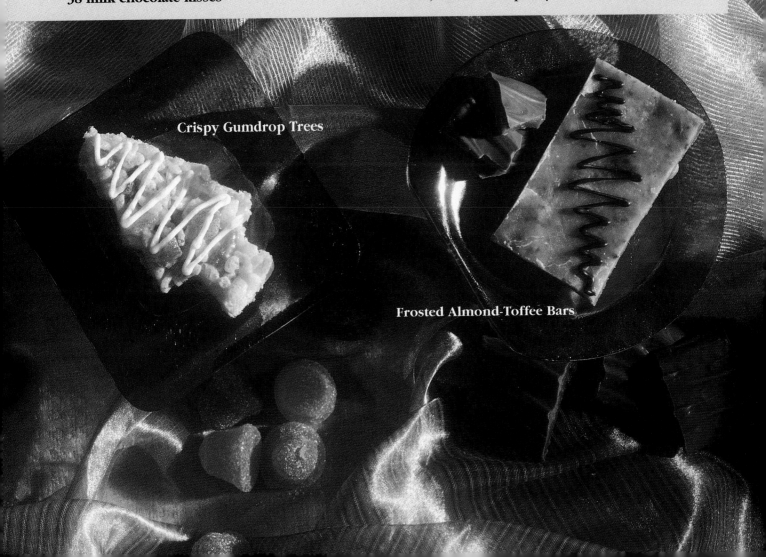

Crispy Gumdrop Trees

Frosted Almond-Toffee Bars

Ribbon-Candy Roulage

Crispy Gumdrop Trees

1 (10-ounce) package large marshmallows
¼ cup butter or margarine
6 cups crisp rice cereal
2 cups chopped assorted gumdrops
½ (16-ounce) container ready-to-spread vanilla
    frosting

Combine marshmallows and butter in a large saucepan. Cook over medium-low heat until marshmallows and butter melt, stirring frequently. Combine cereal and gumdrops in a large bowl; toss well. Pour marshmallow mixture over cereal mixture; stir well. Press mixture into a lightly greased 15- x 10- x 1-inch jellyroll pan; cool completely. Cut into shapes, using a 3½-inch Christmas tree–shaped cookie cutter.

Spoon frosting into a small heavy-duty, zip-top plastic bag; seal bag. Snip a tiny hole in 1 corner of bag, using scissors; pipe frosting onto trees in a decorative design. Yield: 30 cookies.

Frosted Almond-Toffee Bars

1 cup butter or margarine, softened
1 cup firmly packed brown sugar
2 cups all-purpose flour
½ teaspoon baking powder
¼ teaspoon salt
1½ tablespoons instant coffee granules
1 cup crushed English toffee-flavored candy
    bars
2 (2-ounce) packages slivered almonds, toasted
1 cup sifted powdered sugar
2 tablespoons milk
1 tablespoon butter or margarine, softened
1 teaspoon vanilla extract
2 (1-ounce) squares semisweet chocolate

Beat butter at medium speed of an electric mixer until creamy; gradually add brown sugar, beating well. Combine flour and next 3 ingredients; add to butter mixture, beating just until blended. Stir in crushed candy bars and almonds. Spread mixture into a greased 15- x 10- x 1-inch jellyroll pan. Bake at 350° for 18 minutes or until lightly browned. Combine powdered sugar and next 3 ingredients; spread over warm bars. Cool in pan on a wire rack. Cut into bars.

Place chocolate in a heavy-duty, zip-top plastic bag; seal bag. Submerge bag in hot water until chocolate melts. Snip a tiny hole in 1 corner of bag, using scissors; drizzle chocolate over bars. Yield: 32 bars.

Ribbon-Candy Roulage

1 cup sifted cake flour
1/8 teaspoon baking powder
Dash of salt
3 large eggs
3 egg yolks
1/2 cup sugar
1 teaspoon vanilla extract
1/4 cup vegetable oil
3 tablespoons powdered sugar
1/2 cup red currant jelly
Sour Cream Filling and Frosting (see recipe)
Ribbon candy

Grease an 18- x 12- x 1-inch jellyroll pan. Line bottom of pan with waxed paper; grease and flour waxed paper. Set aside.

Sift together first 3 ingredients; set aside.

Beat eggs and egg yolks at high speed of an electric mixer until foamy; continue to beat, adding sugar in a slow, steady stream. Beat 3 to 4 minutes or until mixture is thick, pale, and tripled in volume. Stir in vanilla.

Fold flour mixture into egg mixture gradually. Transfer one-third of batter to a small bowl; add oil, stirring with a wire whisk until blended. Add to remaining batter, stirring to blend. Spread batter in pan. Bake at 350° for 12 minutes or until cake is lightly browned and springs back when touched in center.

Sift powdered sugar in an 18- x 12-inch rectangle on a cloth towel. When cake is done, immediately turn out onto sugared towel. Peel off waxed paper. Starting at narrow end, roll up cake in towel; cool on a wire rack, seam side down.

Place jelly in a small saucepan. Cook over medium-low heat until melted, stirring frequently. Unroll cake, and remove towel. Brush cake with melted jelly.

Spread 1¾ cups Sour Cream Filling and Frosting over jelly. Reroll cake, and place on a serving plate, seam side down. Spread remaining sour cream mixture over cake. Cover loosely, and chill. Arrange ribbon candy on top of cake before serving. Cut into slices to serve. Yield: 10 servings.

Sour Cream Filling and Frosting

1½ cups whipping cream
⅔ cup sour cream
⅓ cup sifted powdered sugar
2 teaspoons vanilla extract
3 tablespoons crushed ribbon candy

Combine first 4 ingredients in a chilled bowl; beat at medium-high speed of an electric mixer 3 to 4 minutes or until stiff peaks form. For filling, transfer 1¾ cups mixture to a small bowl; fold in crushed candy. For frosting, use remaining mixture. Yield: 4 cups.

Dandy Ribbon Candy

Ribbon candy is an old holiday treat. These days, while it's likely to be made by machine, one confectioner still keeps a hand on tradition.

Candy connoisseurs relish the handmade offerings of Hammond Candy Company in Denver, Colorado. Since 1920 the Hammond family has produced traditional treats, including hard-to-find ribbon candy. Emery Dorsey, Hammond's chief candy maker, turns out thousands of pounds of the sweet, striped ribbon candy each year.

Lucky Denver residents snap up quantities of the candy, but from October to May, Hammond's also ships sweets to fans around the country. For a price list, see the source listing on page 157.

Triple-Treat Bars

Triple-Treat Bars

Vegetable cooking spray
1 (12-ounce) package butterscotch morsels
   (2 cups)
½ cup plus 2 tablespoons creamy peanut butter
4 cups granola
1½ cups candy-coated chocolate pieces

Coat a 13- x 9- x 2-inch pan with cooking spray; line with waxed paper.

Combine butterscotch morsels and peanut butter in top of a double boiler; bring water to a boil. Reduce heat to low; cook until morsels melt.

Combine granola and chocolate pieces in a bowl; pour butterscotch mixture over granola mixture, stirring to coat. Spread mixture in prepared pan. Cover and chill until firm. Cut into bars. Yield: 18 bars.

Cinnamon-Spiced Cider

1 gallon apple cider
1 cup red cinnamon candies
1 orange, thinly sliced
2 tablespoons frozen lemonade concentrate

Combine all ingredients in a Dutch oven. Bring to a boil; reduce heat, and simmer, uncovered, 30 minutes, stirring occasionally. Serve hot. Yield: 1 gallon.

Cinnamon-Spiced Cider

Great Gifts to Go

Homemade goodies make terrific gifts. For pretty, practical packaging, consider these containers:

• **Papier-mâché boxes.** Brown-paper boxes are inexpensive, come in a variety of sizes, and are widely available at hobby and homes stores.

• **Time-honored tins.** Cookie and cracker tins are traditional favorites for packaging foods. Buy new tins at kitchen shops, or shop flea markets and garage sales for vintage tins.

• **Kitchen aids.** Check out restaurant-supply and kitchen stores for aluminum pudding molds, square cake pans, pie plates, bread pans, and ice cream molds. They make unusual containers, and they'll be useful long after your cookies have been reduced to crumbs.

• **Paper lunch sacks.** Gather crayons, markers, stickers, glitter paints, paint pens, and ribbons—whatever is in your children's art-supply boxes. Then invite the kids to decorate their own sassy gift sacks for teachers and friends.

HOST'S HOLIDAY: AN EASY WINE AND CHEESE BUFFET

Want to throw a fantastic Christmas party but feel pressed for time? Our easy plan for a no-cook buffet is just the answer. We've organized everything: a great menu that serves 24, shopping and supplies lists, and step-by-step directions for a buffet that's bountiful as well as beautiful.

Menu

Chutney-Topped Brie with Baguette Slices
Mozzarella Sticks with Marinara Sauce
Herbed Cream Cheese–Spinach Spread with Crudités
LeRoy Cheese with Peppercorns
Cheese Ball or Port Wine Cheddar
Cheddar Wheels
Layered Cheese Wedge
Summer Sausage with Mustard
Assorted Crackers and Breads
Red and White Wine
Chilled Sparkling Water
Coffee

Making a List, Checking It Twice

The following lists organize the items you'll need for the party. If convenience is most important to you, buy paper napkins, plastic wine glasses, plates, and cutlery. If you want to keep costs down, use your own tableware and borrow what you don't have. (In fact, if you and a friend join forces to co-host the party, you can cut all your costs in half.)

Party Supplies

- at least 24 wine glasses
- 16 to 24 water glasses
- 6 to 12 coffee cups
- 24 to 36 plates
- 48 cocktail napkins
- 7 to 10 serving platters or cutting boards
- 5 or 6 serving bowls
- place cards for identifying cheeses (optional)
- cheese knives
- wooden picks in several small holders
- corkscrew

Greens and Things

- boughs of greenery
- large piece of fabric for tablecloth
- tall, narrow container for centerpiece
- several containers or decorative items, such as terra-cotta pots, garden ornaments, food tins, hurricane lamps, etc., for creating height at center of buffet
- votives and several candles with candlesticks

Market List

- 1 (2-pound) wheel Brie cheese
- 2 (1-pound) wheels Cheddar cheese
- 1 pound mozzarella cheese
- 2 (6½-ounce) containers herbed cream cheese–spinach spread
- 1 (12-ounce) wedge LeRoy cheese with peppercorns
- 1 (1-pound) cheese ball or 1 (8-ounce) container port wine Cheddar cheese
- 1 (12-ounce) wedge layered cheese (such as Double Gloucester and Stilton)
- 4 French baguettes, sliced
- 5 round loaves assorted breads (such as wheat, pumpernickel, sourdough)
- 4 to 6 boxes assorted breadsticks and crackers (such as water crackers, buttery crackers, biscotti)
- 1 (8-ounce) stick summer sausage
- 1 (8-ounce) jar Dijon and/or honey mustard
- 1 (9-ounce) jar chutney
- 1 (26-ounce) jar marinara sauce
- 2 bunches broccoli
- 1 bunch carrots with tops
- 4 sweet red peppers
- 2 bunches celery
- assorted fruits and herbs for garnishes and display
- 3 bottles red wine (such as pinot noir and cabernet)
- 3 bottles white wine (such as sauvignon blanc and fumé blanc)
- 4 (25-ounce) or 10 (11-ounce) bottles sparkling water
- coffee with sugar and half-and-half

1 To create height at the center of the buffet, place greenery in a tall, narrow container. Around the container, arrange decorative accessories of varying heights. Some of the pieces should have flat tops to support bowls or platters of food.

HOW TO BUILD A

2 Continue building the center of the buffet, mix-ing decorative items among the trays and bowls for food. Substitute pieces as desired, placing tall ones at the center and flat ones at the edge.

3 About an hour before the party, begin adding the food, evenly spacing the cheese selections along the length of the table.

BOUNTIFUL BUFFET

4 Add the rest of the food, filling in gaps with fruit or whole loaves of bread. Set up beverages in a separate area so guests can move about easily.

GEM OF A SETTING

Bejeweled dinnerware makes for a setting that sparkles with holiday spirit. Pick up glass gems at an import or hobby shop and plain ceramic dinnerware at a restaurant-supply store, and you can put together your own designer creations for just a few dollars.

Materials for 2 candle bobeches, 4 chargers, and 4 napkin rings:
2 white ceramic bobeches (see Note below)
4 white ceramic chargers
4 napkin rings
Approx. 125 (½"- to ¾"-diameter) multicolored glass gems with flat backs (see Note below)
clear silicone glue
masking tape (optional)

Note: To substitute clear glass bobeches (candle collars that catch dripping wax), paint the underside of the bobeches with white acrylic paint. For sources for glass gems, see page 157.

1. Wash items. Wash bobeches, dinnerware, and gems in warm, sudsy water; rinse and dry thoroughly.

2. Decorate bobeches. Glue 5 gems on top of each bobeche.

3. Decorate napkin rings. If rings have flat backs, glue 3 gems on top of each ring. If rings are round, evenly space and glue gems around entire ring.

4. Decorate chargers. Evenly space and glue gems around rim of each charger.

5. Let dry. If desired, stabilize gems with thin strips of masking tape. Silicone glue dries to touch in 1 hour and cures in 24 hours.

It's a Wash

Once the glue has cured properly, the projects are dishwasher safe. We've washed our pieces dozens of times, and they still look great.

An Ornamental Tablecloth

**Trim your holiday table with a garland of dancing ornaments.
It's easy when you machine-appliqué a purchased tablecloth with
ornaments cut from jazzy dish towels.**

Materials:
1 (72" x 110") red-and-white striped tablecloth
Various plaid or jacquard dish towels or tea
  towels (see Note below)
Tracing paper
2 yards 17"-wide paper-backed fusible web
Water-soluble marker
7½ yards green jumbo rickrack
Liquid ravel preventer
Thread: green, black, plus colors to match dish
  towels
2 yards 22"-wide tear-away stabilizer

Note: Tablecloth shown in photograph has 36 ornaments. Appliqué ornaments were cut from 14 different 20" x 28" towels. You can, however, cut as many as 12 appliqués from 1 towel. Adjust quantity of rickrack, fusible web, and stabilizer to suit size of tablecloth you select. If desired, buy additional towels to use as oversize napkins. For source listing for tablecloth and towels used here, see page 157.

1. Pretreat materials. Wash, dry, and press tablecloth and towels.

2. Make ornament pattern. Select a large glass or other round object with a diameter of 4" to 5"; trace around object on tracing paper and cut out.

3. Cut out ornament shapes. Transfer ornament pattern to paper side of web 36 times. (You may choose to have fewer or more ornaments on your tablecloth.) Roughly cut out shapes slightly larger than drawn. Following manufacturer's instructions, fuse web shapes to wrong side of towels. Cut out shapes along marked lines and remove paper backing. Set aside.

4. Attach rickrack garland. Spread tablecloth on table. Using water-soluble marker, mark cloth where it drops off each edge of table.

Pin rickrack to cloth in 1 continuous piece, snaking

it back and forth across marked lines and curving around corners. To finish ends, trim excess, leaving ½" allowance on each end. Apply liquid ravel preventer; let dry. Turn ½" under on each end and then abut folded ends. Stitch along center of rickrack.

5. Fuse ornament shapes. Referring to photograph, on right side of tablecloth, randomly place shapes approximately 1½" below garland. Cluster or overlap some shapes. Fuse shapes to tablecloth.

6. Stitch ornament shapes. Cut stabilizer into 36 (6") squares. On wrong side of tablecloth, center 1 stabilizer square under each shape. Using matching thread and medium satin stitch, stitch around each shape (see Diagram). For cap, using wide satin stitch, stitch 2 rows to form approximately 1"-long rectangle, varying placement of cap so that some ornaments appear to be at an angle.

7. Mark and stitch hooks. When all shapes have been appliquéd in place, use water-soluble marker to draw hook from each ornament cap to rickrack. Using black thread and narrow satin stitch, stitch along marked hooks (see Diagram). Remove stabilizer.

DIAGRAM

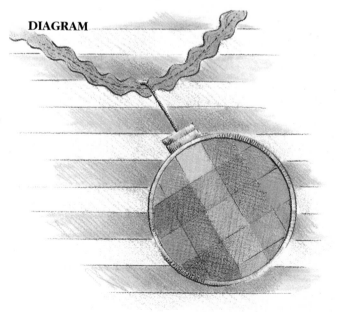

SEASONED GREETINGS

Spice blends make quick gifts from the kitchen. As a thoughtful touch,
tie them off with gift tags bearing serving suggestions. And here's a bonus
for the cook: If you buy your whole spices and jars in bulk, spicy isn't pricey.

Southwestern Blend

¼ cup dried parsley flakes
¼ cup dried oregano
2 tablespoons dried thyme
2 tablespoons cumin seeds
1 tablespoon black peppercorns
1 teaspoon paprika
3 dried red chile pepper pods

Place all ingredients in a mini food processor or coffee grinder; process until spices are blended and peppercorns are a medium grind. Yield: ½ cup.

Fajita Marinade: Combine ¼ cup vegetable oil, 2 tablespoons lime juice, 1 tablespoon Southwestern Blend, 1 teaspoon minced garlic, and ¼ teaspoon salt; pour over 1 pound flank steak or chicken breast strips. Cover and marinate in refrigerator one hour.

Zesty Black Beans: Cook ⅓ cup finely chopped onion in 2 teaspoons vegetable oil over medium-high heat until tender; stir in 2 teaspoons Southwestern Blend. Add 1 (15-ounce) can black beans, drained; partially mash beans. Serve with sour cream, shredded Monterey Jack cheese, or chopped tomato.

Apple Spice Blend

12 (3-inch) sticks cinnamon
8 whole cloves
3 whole nutmegs
1 teaspoon whole allspice

Place all ingredients in a mini food processor or coffee grinder; process until finely ground. Yield: ½ cup.

Spice It Up: Stir Apple Spice Blend into applesauce, oatmeal, or French toast batter.

Top Topping: Combine equal parts Apple Spice Blend and sugar; sprinkle over sugar cookie dough before baking or buttered bread before toasting.

Garam Masala

4 (3-inch) sticks cinnamon
3 bay leaves, crumbled
2 tablespoons black peppercorns
1 tablespoon plus 1 teaspoon cumin seeds
1 teaspoon cardamom seeds
1 teaspoon whole cloves
2 teaspoons freshly grated nutmeg

Break cinnamon sticks into small pieces. Heat a skillet over medium-high heat; add cinnamon stick pieces and next 5 ingredients. Cook 3 to 5 minutes, stirring constantly, until spices become fragrant. Remove from heat; let cool. Place spices and nutmeg in a mini food processor or coffee grinder; process until finely ground. Yield: about ⅓ cup.

Grilled Lamb: Rub Garam Masala over surface of a butterflied leg of lamb before grilling.

Quick Chicken Curry: Cook 1 medium onion, sliced, in 1 tablespoon hot vegetable oil over medium-high heat, stirring constantly, until tender. Add 4 cups chopped cooked chicken; 2 medium potatoes, diced; 1 (14½-ounce) can diced tomatoes, undrained; 1 cup water; and 1 tablespoon Garam Masala. Bring to a boil; cover, reduce heat, and simmer 15 to 20 minutes or until potato is tender. Serve over hot cooked rice.

Quick Jambalaya with Creole Blend

Creole Blend

¼ cup dried parsley flakes
3 tablespoons dried celery flakes
3 tablespoons dried thyme
2 tablespoons dried oregano
2 tablespoons freeze-dried chives
1 tablespoon black peppercorns
1 teaspoon paprika
4 bay leaves
3 dried red chile peppers

Place all ingredients in a mini food processor or coffee grinder; process until finely ground. Yield: ½ cup.

Dip with Zip: Combine ½ cup mayonnaise, ½ cup sour cream, ¼ cup minced green onions, ¼ cup minced green pepper, 1 teaspoon Creole Blend, ¼ teaspoon garlic salt, and ¼ teaspoon hot sauce. Cover and chill at least 2 hours. Serve with fresh vegetables.

Quick Jambalaya: Cook 1 cup chopped onion, ½ cup chopped green pepper, and ½ pound sliced smoked sausage in 1 tablespoon vegetable oil over medium-high heat, stirring constantly, until vegetables are tender. Stir in 1 (14½-ounce) can ready-to-serve chicken broth, 1 (14½-ounce) can diced tomatoes, 1½ cups chopped cooked chicken, 1 cup uncooked long-grain rice, and 1 tablespoon Creole Blend. Bring to a boil; reduce heat, and simmer, uncovered, 25 minutes or until liquid is absorbed and rice is tender.

Taste of Tuscany

¼ cup dried sage
¼ cup dried rosemary
1 teaspoon salt
½ teaspoon black peppercorns

Place all ingredients in a mini food processor or coffee grinder; process until finely ground. Yield: ½ cup.

Italian Crostini: Slice a 1-pound French baguette into ½-inch-thick slices. Brush cut surfaces with olive oil, and rub with a garlic clove. Combine 4 ounces softened goat cheese or cream cheese and 1 teaspoon Taste of Tuscany; spread over slices. Top with roasted red pepper strips. Broil until lightly browned. Serve immediately.

Italian Crostini with Taste of Tuscany

Savory Roasted Potatoes: Coat 1 pound new potatoes with olive oil; add 1 teaspoon kosher salt, 1 teaspoon Taste of Tuscany, and 1 clove garlic, crushed. Toss gently. Bake potatoes at 400° for 30 minutes or until tender and lightly browned.

Wild Game Mix

2 tablespoons dried thyme
1 tablespoon black peppercorns
2 teaspoons fennel seeds
16 juniper berries
3 bay leaves

Place all ingredients in a mini food processor or coffee grinder; process until mixture is a fine powder. Yield: about ⅓ cup.

Venison Marinade: Combine ½ cup dry red wine, 2 tablespoons olive oil, 1½ tablespoons Worcestershire sauce, and 1 teaspoon Wild Game Mix. Pour over 6 (4- to 6-ounce) bacon-wrapped boneless venison filets. Cover and marinate in refrigerator at least 8 hours.

Flavorful Buffalo Burgers: Combine 1 pound ground buffalo, 2 tablespoons minced onion, 2 tablespoons Worcestershire sauce, and 1 teaspoon Wild Game Mix. Shape mixture into 4 patties. Grill or pan-fry as desired.

Classic French Flavors

12 bay leaves
¼ cup dried thyme
¼ cup dried parsley flakes
2 tablespoons dried tarragon
2 tablespoons dried basil
1 teaspoon black peppercorns
1 teaspoon dried lemon peel

Place all ingredients in a mini food processor or coffee grinder; process until finely ground. Yield: ⅓ cup.

Classic French Vinaigrette: Combine ⅔ cup olive oil, ⅓ cup red wine vinegar, 1 tablespoon Dijon mustard, 2 teaspoons Classic French Flavors, ¼ teaspoon salt, ¼ teaspoon sugar, and 1 clove garlic, crushed, in a jar. Cover tightly, and shake vigorously. Serve with salad greens, or toss with cooked new potatoes for potato salad. Yield: 1 cup.

Herb Butter: Combine ½ cup softened butter and ¾ teaspoon Classic French Flavors. Serve with grilled fish or chicken.

Make It Easy

- **Shopping Express.** If you buy ingredients and containers by mail, you save time and money; see page 157 for source listings.
- **In Keeping with Good Taste.** You can freeze whole dried spices up to three years and ground seasonings up to six months.

  After you make the spice blends, store them in airtight containers in a cool, dry place. Keep them away from cooktops, ovens, and dishwashers, since heat speeds deterioration.
- **A Clean Machine.** To remove spice residue from your mini food processor or coffee grinder, process small batches of granulated sugar until the sugar remains white. This method also works for removing particles left over from grinding flavored coffees.
- **Tags in a Snap.** With a rubber stamp, you can quickly knock out dozens of gift tags. (We made the tags on page 102 large enough for our serving suggestions to be written on the back.)

  Stamps in a variety of designs—including holiday designs and large borders perfect for making tags—are now widely available at craft stores and stationery shops. For a source listing for the stamps we used, see page 157.

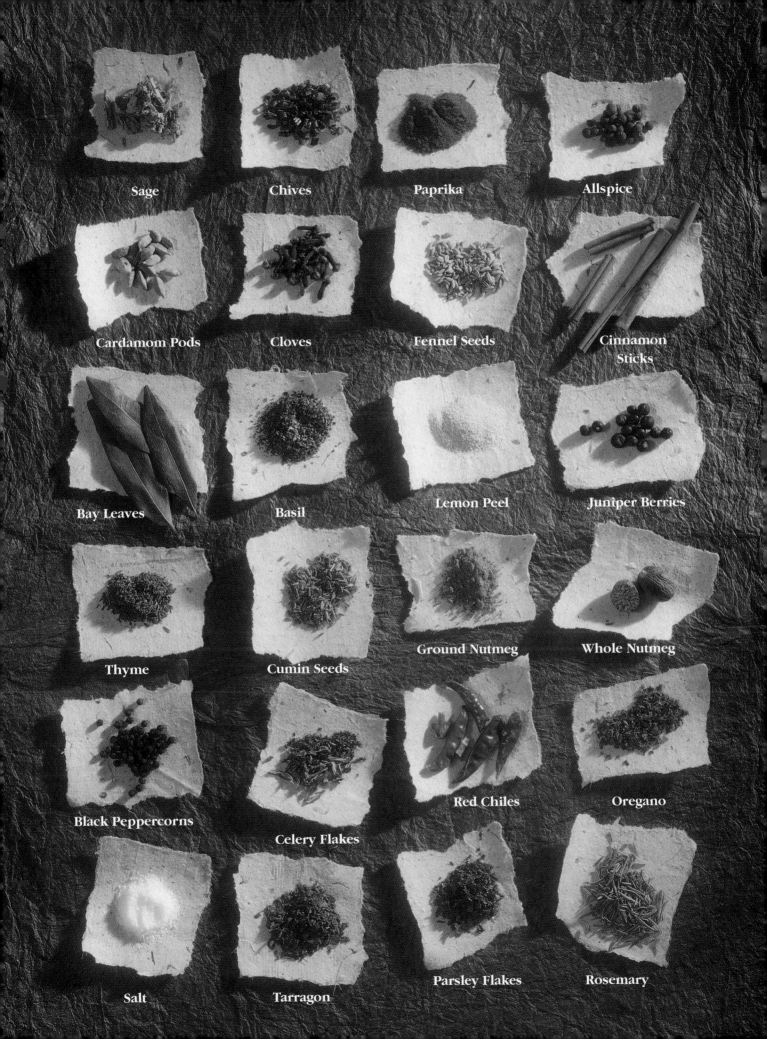

Sage

Chives

Paprika

Allspice

Cardamom Pods

Cloves

Fennel Seeds

Cinnamon
Sticks

Bay Leaves

Basil

Lemon Peel

Juniper Berries

Thyme

Cumin Seeds

Ground Nutmeg

Whole Nutmeg

Black Peppercorns

Celery Flakes

Red Chiles

Oregano

Salt

Tarragon

Parsley Flakes

Rosemary

IDEAS

SWEETS IN SECONDS

Go ahead—host a coffee klatch for the gang, make dessert for the office party, invite the neighbors over for a nightcap. With our collection of speedy sweets—each one containing just five or fewer ingredients—indulging friends is as easy as pie.

Ambrosia Pudding Parfait

Country Fruit Crisp

Golden Almond Ice Cream Balls

Country Fruit Crisp

Pour 2 (21-ounce) cans apple pie filling into a 10- x 6- x 2-inch baking dish; top with 1½ cups fresh or frozen (thawed) cranberries. Combine 1 cup crushed miniature cheese-filled round sandwich crackers, ⅓ cup firmly packed brown sugar, and 3 tablespoons softened butter or margarine; sprinkle over apple mixture.

Bake at 350° for 30 to 40 minutes or until bubbly. Serve warm. Yield: 8 servings.

Ambrosia Pudding Parfait

Peel and section 2 oranges; combine with 1 (8-ounce) can unsweetened pineapple tidbits (undrained). Layer fruit mixture, 4 (4-ounce) cartons vanilla pudding, and 8 crumbled macaroons in 4 (6-ounce) parfait glasses. Serve immediately. Yield: 4 servings.

Eggnog Bread Pudding

Tear 8 (1-ounce) slices raisin bread into bite-size pieces; divide evenly among 4 (10-ounce) lightly greased custard cups. Combine 1⅓ cups eggnog and 1 tablespoon bourbon; pour ⅓ cup eggnog mixture into each custard cup.

Bake at 325° for 25 to 27 minutes or until lightly browned. Let stand 10 minutes before serving. Serve with hard sauce or whipped cream sprinkled with ground cinnamon. Yield: 4 servings.

Golden Almond Ice Cream Balls

Scoop 1 pint vanilla ice cream into 4 balls; freeze until firm. Process 1 (6-ounce) can honey-roasted almonds and ½ cup flaked coconut in a food processor or blender until finely chopped. Roll ice cream balls in almond mixture, and freeze until firm. Combine ¼ cup honey and ¼ cup amaretto; drizzle over ice cream balls just before serving. Yield: 4 servings.

Irish Cream Shake

Combine 3½ cups coffee or chocolate ice cream, ¼ cup milk, ¼ cup chocolate syrup, and 3 tablespoons Irish cream liqueur in an electric blender; process until smooth, stopping once to scrape down sides. Serve immediately. Yield: 3½ cups.

Pumpkin Mousse with Cinnamon Cream

Combine 1 (16-ounce) container ready-to-spread vanilla frosting, 1 (8-ounce) carton sour cream, and 1 cup canned pumpkin, stirring with a wire whisk until smooth.

Reserve ½ cup of 1 (8-ounce) container frozen whipped topping (thawed); fold remaining whipped topping into pumpkin mixture. Spoon mixture evenly into 6 dessert dishes. Combine reserved whipped topping and ¼ teaspoon ground cinnamon; dollop on each serving. Yield: 6 servings.

Instructions for gift bags begin on page 114.

PLEASURES OF THE SEASON

Round out your holiday crafting with gift bags of patterned velvet—and find that special link between giving and receiving. Friends and family will love everything you've made for them. And the satisfaction of creating will be all yours.

Instructions for these and other projects are on page 115.

THE VELVET TOUCH

If Christmas has a favorite fabric, it must be velvet.
Imprinting it with exuberant whirls and swirls is simple—
all you need are an iron and a few cardboard cutouts.

1. Make templates. Gather tracing paper, carbon paper, mat board, scissors or craft knife, 100% rayon velvet, spray starch, and iron. Using tracing paper, trace desired patterns on page 146. Using carbon paper, transfer patterns to mat board; cut out templates.

2. Arrange templates. On ironing board, arrange templates in desired pattern. Place velvet (pile side down) on templates. Spray back of velvet with a medium-to-heavy coat of starch and allow to soak into fabric.

3. Heat-set pattern. To find hottest iron setting that won't scorch velvet, experiment by ironing a scrap of velvet. Using this setting, iron area of velvet covering templates. Let velvet cool in place.

4. Check results. If velvet did not imprint well, carefully replace velvet on templates, aligning edges of imprints with edges of templates; iron again. Repeat steps 2–4 to imprint rest of velvet.

For a lark of a scarf, line a rectangle of velvet with faille or silk and whipstitch fringe to the ends. For source listing for velvet and trim, see page 157.

For an ornament, cut a velvet square to cover a Styrofoam ball. Finish the edges with a narrow zigzag and secure with a ribbon bow. For the gift bags on pages 112–13, use the same method to finish the edges of a narrow rectangle of velvet before stitching side seams.

To make a store-bought album special, disassemble the album and use fabric glue to cover the spine, front, and back with imprinted velvet; reassemble album. For the frame shown on page 112, use the same method to cover a purchased frame.

A Winter Wonder-Man

For designer Patrick Lose, there's no time like snow time. Christmas—with all its trimmings—is still his favorite season.

Even now, when Patrick's career as a crafts designer has taken him in so many directions, Christmas is always a source of inspiration.

It's been that way since 1988, when a magazine published some of his holiday projects. Readers liked his colorful take on folk art—an approach he calls "contemporary primitive"—and his new career took off.

Since then, Patrick has created patterns for crafts, clothing, and home-decorating accessories, and his sidelines include printed fabrics, dolls, greeting cards, and other licensed products.

Today, while Patrick designs whatever strikes his fancy, Christmas is still a favored theme. "I love everything about Christmas," he says, "except for the fact that it comes and goes so quickly. For a few weeks out of the year, people become a little more focused on what's really important in life."

For Patrick, the oldest of eight children and the proud father of 12-year-old Katie, that means family and friends. Everyone gathers to celebrate traditions old and new, and Katie cheerfully joins in whatever the schedule holds—whether it's shopping for gifts, watching reruns of "The Grinch Who Stole Christmas," or modeling her father's designs (see page 119).

To each holiday design Patrick brings that same spirit of warmth, innocence, and plain old fun. He likes to take the traditional and make it whimsical—hence the name of his business, Out on a Whim.

And lest things get predictable, Patrick gives a single design several forms. For a perfect example, turn to the following pages, where his starstruck angel finds more than one way to herald the holidays.

117

THREE ANGLES ON AN ANGEL

Patrick Lose believes in giving crafters choices. Here he's taken one of his designs— a friendly folk art angel—and translated it into three techniques. Short on time? Shoot for his star pins on page 121.

Cutout-Trimmed Wreath

Materials:
Patterns on pages 142–43
11" x 17" piece of ¼"-thick pine, poplar, or
   birch plywood
Tracing paper
Scroll saw and #5 blade
100-grit sandpaper
Acrylic paints: red, green, gold, ivory, beige,
   rust
Paintbrush
Acrylic spray finish
18"- to 24"-diameter vine wreath
Wood glue

1. Transfer pattern. Using tracing paper and pencil, reverse pattern and transfer angel (omitting background and border) and 3 separate stars to wood.

2. Cut out and paint designs. Using saw, cut out designs and sand smooth. Referring to photograph for colors, paint designs; let dry. Apply spray finish; let dry.

3. Attach designs. Referring to photograph for placement, glue angel and stars to wreath.

No-Sew Appliqué Pullover

Materials:
Patterns on pages 142–43
⅓ yard paper-backed fusible web
Fine-tip permanent markers: black, brown
Fabric scraps: royal blue, red, red-and-green
   stripe, green, gold, ivory, beige, rust, purple
White 100%-cotton pullover
Gold glitter fabric paint with applicator tip

Note: Before beginning, wash, dry, and press pullover and fabric scraps to remove sizing.

1. Transfer patterns. Lay web (paper side up) on patterns. Using black marker, transfer individual patterns for 1 angel (complete with background and border) and 5 separate stars to paper side of web. Cutting ½" outside pattern lines, cut out pieces.

2. Fuse pieces. Following manufacturer's instructions, fuse web to wrong side of fabric scraps. Let cool. Cut out appliqué pieces along pattern lines.

Remove paper backing. Referring to photograph and pattern for placement, center background and border pieces on front of pullover; fuse in place. Repeat for angel and then for stars. Using brown marker, mark facial features.

3. Outline pieces. Using fabric paint, outline raw edges of each piece, covering edges completely. Let pullover lie flat for 24 hours before wearing.

To launder pullover, turn wrong side out, wash by hand, and hang to dry.

Appliqué Table Runner

Materials:
Patterns on pages 142–43
1½ yards 45"-wide royal blue fabric
45" x 60" piece cotton batting
Dressmaker's pen
Fabric scraps: red, red-and-green stripe, gold, ivory, beige, rust
⅔ yard paper-backed fusible web
⅓ yard 45"-wide cream cotton duck canvas
Brown fine-tip permanent marker
3¾ yards gold double-fold bias tape
Thread to match fabrics

Note: Before beginning, wash, dry, and press fabrics to remove sizing. Seam allowances are ½".

1. Cut out blue fabric. From royal blue fabric, cut 2 (13" x 45") rectangles. Stack rectangles; referring to photograph, trim short ends to form points. Using 1 blue piece as a pattern, cut a piece of batting to match.

2. Transfer patterns. Lay web (paper side up) on patterns. Using dressmaker's pen, transfer individual patterns for 2 angels (omit background and border) and 5 separate stars to paper side of web. Cutting ½" outside pattern lines, cut out pieces.

3. Fuse appliqué pieces. Following manufacturer's instructions, fuse web pieces to wrong side of fabric scraps. Let cool. Cut out appliqué pieces along pattern lines. Remove paper backing. Fuse pieces to right side of canvas.

Fuse web to wrong side of canvas, behind appliqué pieces. Let cool.

Cut out appliqué pieces along raw edges. Remove paper backing from web.

On 1 end of 1 blue fabric piece, arrange pieces for 1 angel, centering feet 3" from point and referring to photograph and pattern for placement of remaining pieces. Fuse in place. Repeat for opposite end.

Arrange 5 extra stars as desired along center of blue fabric. Fuse in place. With brown marker, mark facial features.

4. Stitch table runner. Stack plain blue fabric piece (right side down), batting, and top (right side up), aligning raw edges. Baste in place. With right sides facing and raw edges aligned, stitch bias tape around all edges of top, mitering tape at points. Fold tape to back and slipstitch in place. Press.

Thread bobbin with royal blue thread. Using top thread to match each appliqué piece and a narrow satin stitch, machine-stitch around raw edges of appliqués.

Dancing Star Pins

Materials for 1 pin:
Pattern on page 143
Tracing paper
Scrap of ¼"-thick pine, poplar, or birch
   plywood
Scroll saw and #5 blade
100-grit sandpaper
Spray paint: red, green, or gold
Pin back
Craft glue
Gold glitter paint with applicator tip

1. Cut out star. Using tracing paper, transfer pattern to wood. Using saw, cut out star. Sand star smooth.

2. Paint star. Spray-paint star on both sides, letting paint dry between applications.

3. Attach pin back. Center and glue pin back on 1 side of star.

4. Decorate star. Referring to photograph, outline star with glitter paint; then paint random dots inside outline. Let dry.

Bolts from the Blue

Patrick's two lines of fabrics are a success on two fronts. Crafters have discovered that the yard goods—with their bold colors and energetic patterns—pack a lot of punch. And for Patrick they're a proud achievement.

"Designing my own line of fabrics is really a dream come true for me," he says. "It's been a goal ever since I was creating costumes for community theaters." But as time passed and other projects came up, his hopes faded.

A chance meeting between his pattern distributor and a fabric buyer changed all that. The buyer liked Patrick's designs and asked, "Do you think this guy would ever consider designing fabrics?"

That was all Patrick needed. Within weeks he completed a set of original illustrations ready for printing. Later, when the orders came flooding in, the fabric company tripled its print run. And Patrick immediately began planning his second line.

His first series—"Out on a Whim"—is named after his business and showcases his distinctive approach to folk art style. Colors are pure and bright. Stars and squiggles are full of energy. Stripes and checks are wavy and look handpainted.

His second line—"For the Holidays"—is a boon for Christmas crafters. Dancing ornaments in vibrant colors are the most popular motifs. Backgrounds and coordinated fabrics are marbleized, striped, or checked. There's also a set of fabrics for Halloween and the Fourth of July.

Because most of his fabrics are printed in intense, saturated colors, Patrick recommends washing them in cold water with the gentle cycle and then drying them at low heat.

For more information on Out on a Whim patterns and fabrics, see page 157.

PRESENTS THAT PAMPER

Herbal bath oils, salts, and soaps are wonderful gifts. But if you've bought any lately, you know they can be costly. We asked author Janice Cox for alternatives, with splendid results—luxurious, easy-to-make bath products that won't break the bank.

When it comes to devising practical alternatives for commercial products, Janice is a pro. For nearly 20 years, this Medford, Oregon, woman has made her own cosmetics, some of them from recipes handed down through three generations of her family. Janice's book, *Natural Beauty at Home: More Than 200 Easy-to-Use Recipes for Body, Bath, and Hair,* has just been published, and she was glad to create for our readers a collection of botanical bath oils, relaxing salts, and handmade soaps.

Before You Begin

Here are some of Janice's tips to help you get started:

• The recipes that follow use common ingredients often sold at the grocery store or pharmacy.

• For dried herbs and flowers, check out crafts and homes stores. Or gather them fresh from your garden or local farmers' markets, and dry them yourself.

• For essential oils and castile soap, go to a health food store or bath shop, or see the source listings on page 157.

• The cheapest containers are glass bottles and jars you recycle from your own pantry. Department stores and kitchen shops often carry inexpensive spice jars and decorative bottles with cork stoppers. Kitchen shops also sell cork stoppers separately.

• Once you've gathered your materials, just prepare the recipes on the following pages.

Botanical Bath Oils

• The following recipes call for the oils used to make products shown in the photographs at right, but you can easily make substitutions. We used avocado, almond, and mineral oils, but you can also use safflower, sunflower, and olive oils. Mineral oil has the longest shelf life.

• To allow the bath oils to blend, let them sit for two weeks before gift giving. Store them in a cool, dark, dry place, since heat and light can alter their color and composition.

• The following recipes call for dried herbs and flowers, but other possibilities are dried citrus peel, seashells, colored pebbles, or glass stones.

Chamomile Bath Oil

Materials for 1 bottle:
Clean, dry bottle with cork stopper
**Pesticide-free dried herbs or flowers, such as
   yarrow flowers, safflowers, or strawflowers**
Enough avocado oil to fill bottle
Funnel
Chamomile essential oil
Paraffin
Crayon of desired color
Paintbrush
Scrap of medium-weight paper
Scrap of raffia

   1. Add herbs or flowers. Place desired number of sprigs inside bottle, trimming stems as necessary to fit.

   2. Add oil and fragrance. Using funnel, fill bottle with oil. Add 4 or 5 drops of essential oil for a medium-size (about 16- to 24-ounce) bottle. Insert cork stopper.

   3. Seal bottle. Melt paraffin over low heat; then melt crayon in warm paraffin. Using paintbrush, apply wax around cork and lip of bottle. Invert bottle and dip it into wax several times, letting each coat dry.

   4. Label bottle. For tag, cut scrap of paper into desired shape. Write name of oil on tag. Make a small hole in 1 end of tag. Use raffia to tie tag to bottle.

Chamomile
Bath Oil

Lavender
Bath Oil

Lavender Bath Oil

Materials for 1 bottle:
Clean, dry bottle with cork stopper
**Pesticide-free dried lavender
   and/or rosemary**
Enough mineral oil to fill bottle
Funnel
Lavender essential oil
Paraffin
Crayon of desired color
Paintbrush
Scrap of medium-weight paper
Scrap of raffia

   1. Make and package oil. Repeat steps 1–4 for Chamomile Bath Oil.

Vanilla-Almond Bath Oil

Materials for 1 bottle:
Clean, dry bottle with cork stopper
Pesticide-free dried herbs or flowers,
   such as lavender, globe amaranth,
   rosebuds, or Russian statice
Measuring cup
Funnel
Enough oil—1 part mineral, plus
   1 part almond—to fill bottle
Vanilla essential oil
Paraffin
Crayon of desired color
Paintbrush
Scrap of medium-weight paper
Scrap of raffia

    1. Make and package oil. Repeat steps 1–4 for Chamomile Bath Oil.

Sweet-Grass Bath Oil

Materials for 1 bottle:
Clean, dry bottle with cork stopper
Pesticide-free dried grasses, such as
   sweet grass, quaking grass, or
   other wild grass
Enough almond oil to fill bottle
Funnel
Sweet-grass or rain-scented essential oil
Paraffin
Crayon of desired color
Paintbrush
Scrap of medium-weight paper
Scrap of raffia

    1. Make and package oil. Repeat steps 1–4 for Chamomile Bath Oil.

Rosebud Bath Oil

Materials for 1 bottle:
Clean, dry bottle with cork stopper
Pesticide-free dried flowers or herbs, such as
   rosebuds, lavender, or globe amaranth
Enough mineral oil to fill bottle
Funnel
Rose essential oil
Paraffin
Crayon in desired color
Paintbrush
Scrap of medium-weight paper
Scrap of raffia

    1. Make and package oil. Repeat steps 1–4 for Chamomile Bath Oil.

Vanilla-Almond
Bath Oil
    Rosebud
    Bath Oil
Sweet-Grass
Bath Oil

Scented
Bath Salts

Scented Bath Salts

Materials for 3 cups of bath salts:
Large glass or metal mixing bowl
2 cups Epsom salts
1 cup sea salt or rock salt
Food coloring: green or blue (optional)
¼ teaspoon glycerin (for skin softening)
**Essential oil, such as peppermint, citrus, or
    coconut (for fragrance)**
**Clean, dry jar(s), each with cork stopper or
    metal screw-on lid**

   1. Combine salts. Combine salts in bowl. Mix well.
   2. Add color. If desired, add a few drops of food
coloring and mix well. Continue adding drops of food
coloring until desired shade is achieved. For white
salts, skip this step.
   3. Add glycerin and essential oil. Stir in glycerin
and 4 or 5 drops of essential oil. Mix well.
   4. Package salts. Spoon salts into containers and
seal. Store any leftover salts in an airtight container.

Lavender or Vanilla-Almond Soap

Materials for 6 bars:
6 (3" x 2" x 1") metal cookie cutters for molds
Petroleum jelly
Cookie sheet
Aluminum foil
**6 cups, or about 14 ounces, of shaved,
    unscented white or natural soap,
    such as castile or baby soap (see
    Note below)**
⅓ cup water
Double boiler
**For Lavender Soap: about ¼ cup
    dried lavender flowers,
    crumbled**
**For Vanilla-Almond Soap: vanilla
    essential oil, about ¼ cup ground
    almonds**

   Note: To shave bars of soap, use a vegetable
peeler.

1. Prepare molds. Coat inside of molds with petroleum jelly. Cover cookie sheet with foil. Place molds on cookie sheet. Set aside.

2. Melt soap. Combine soap and water in double boiler and melt over medium heat, stirring occasionally. Do not boil.

Soap will at first appear grainy and dry; continue heating and stirring until it has the consistency of pudding.

3. Add fragrance and texture. For Lavender Soap, add lavender flowers. For Vanilla-Almond Soap, add 4 or 5 drops of essential oil and ground almonds. Mix well.

4. Mold soap. Working quickly, fill molds generously (soap will settle, and you can trim excess later).

Gently tap edges of molds to remove air bubbles. Let molds sit for several hours until soap is completely cool.

5. Air-dry soaps. Remove soap from molds. Place on wire rack to air-dry for at least 24 hours. Trim any rough edges with a sharp knife.

Sandalwood or Oatmeal Soap

Materials for 3 cubes of soap:
3 (3"-square) cardboard boxes for molds
Petroleum jelly
Plastic wrap
6 cups, or about 14 ounces, of shaved, unscented white or natural soap, such as castile or baby soap (see Note below)
⅓ cup of water
Double boiler
For Sandalwood Soap: sandalwood essential oil
For Oatmeal Soap: ¼ cup oatmeal

Note: To shave bars of soap, use a vegetable peeler.

1. Prepare molds. Coat inside of boxes with petroleum jelly; then line them with plastic wrap. Set aside.

2. Make soap. To melt soap, repeat Step 2 for Lavender or Vanilla-Almond Soap. For Sandalwood Soap, add 4 or 5 drops of essential oil. For Oatmeal Soap, add oatmeal. Mix well. To mold soap, repeat steps 4–5 for Lavender or Vanilla-Almond Soap.

Sandalwood Soap

Lavender Soap

Oatmeal Soap

Vanilla-Almond Soap

WEE THREE STOCKINGS

These ornaments positively sing, thanks to embroidery stitches worked in vibrant metallic, silk, and cotton threads. Designer Lois Caron made the background fabrics an important part of the designs—so even a beginner will find them quick to stitch.

Snowflake Stocking

Snowflake Stocking

Materials:
Chart and color key on page 150
2 (9") squares red 28-count linen
Embroidery floss (see color key)
Tapestry needles: size 22 for
    Candlelight threads, size 24
    for Wildflowers
9" square lightweight red fabric
    for interlining
Polyester stuffing
1 yard ¹⁄₁₆"-diameter coordinating
    cording
Thread to match fabric and cording
Extra floss to make tassel (see Step
    3) or coordinating purchased
    3" tassel

Note: Finished design is 4¼" x 5¾". All seam allowances are ¼" unless otherwise indicated. For fabric and floss, see source listings on page 157.

1. Stitch design. On 1 linen square, center and work design according to chart and color key. Refer to Embroidery Diagrams on page 131 as needed.

2. Sew ornament. Stack finished design piece (right side up) on interlining fabric, aligning raw edges. Machine-stitch ¼" outside edges of stitched design.

Stack design/interlining piece (right side down) on remaining linen square. Machine-stitch ⅛" inside first stitching line, leaving top of stocking open. Trim excess fabric, cutting just outside first stitching line.

Clip curves and turn. Stuff lightly. Slipstitch top closed, leaving small opening at top left for cording, tassel, and hanger.

Beginning and ending at top left and leaving 1" tails, whipstitch cording to cover seam.

3. Make tassel. Referring to Tassel Diagram, wrap floss around a 3"-long piece of heavy cardboard to make a thick bundle (Figure A).

Thread needle with length of same color floss. Slide needle under 1 end of floss bundle (Figure B).

Pull needle free and knot floss tightly; cut bundle

Flying Colors Stocking

Winter Forest Stocking

at opposite end (Figure C).

Wrap another length of floss several times around bundle and knot to secure (Figure D).

Trim floss ends at top to 1". Trim ends of tassel even.

4. Finish ornament. Cut 8" of remaining cording and fold in half, aligning raw ends. Tuck 1" of raw ends inside opening at top left of stocking. Also tuck in ends of cording and tassel. Slipstitch opening closed, catching hanger, cording, and tassel ends in seam.

TASSEL DIAGRAM

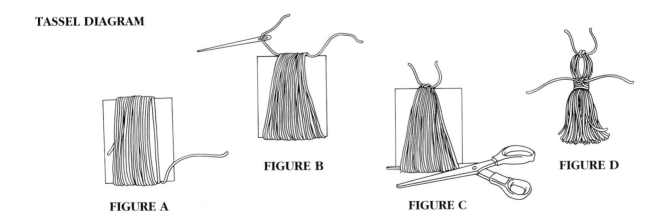

FIGURE A

FIGURE B

FIGURE C

FIGURE D

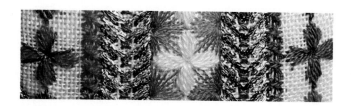

Flying Colors Stocking

Materials:
Chart and color key on page 151
2 (9") squares white 28-count linen
Embroidery floss (see color key)
Tapestry needles: size 22 for Candlelight
    threads, size 24 for Wildflowers and
    Waterlilies threads
9" square lightweight white fabric for
    interlining
Polyester stuffing
1 yard ¹⁄₁₆"-diameter coordinating cording
Thread to match fabric and cording
Extra floss to make tassel or coordinating
    purchased 3" tassel

    Note: Finished design is 4¼" x 5¾". All seam allowances are ¼" unless otherwise indicated. For fabric and floss, see source listings on page 157.
    1. Stitch design. On 1 linen square, center and work design according to chart and color key. Refer to Embroidery Diagrams on page 131 as needed.
    2. Sew ornament. To finish stocking ornament, repeat steps 2–4 for Snowflake Stocking.

Winter Forest Stocking

Materials:
Chart and color key on page 152
2 (9") squares forest green 28-count linen
Embroidery floss (see color key)
Tapestry needles: size 22 for Candlelight
    threads, size 24 for Wildflowers and
    Waterlilies threads
9" square lightweight green fabric for
    interlining
Polyester stuffing
1 yard ¹⁄₁₆"-diameter coordinating cording
Thread to match fabric and cording
Extra floss to make tassel or coordinating
    purchased 3" tassel

    Note: Finished design is 4¼" x 5¾". All seam allowances are ¼" unless otherwise indicated. For fabric and floss, see source listings on page 157.
    1. Stitch design. On 1 linen square, center and work design according to chart and color key. Refer to Embroidery Diagrams on page 131 as needed.
    2. Sew ornament. To finish stocking ornament, repeat steps 2–4 for Snowflake Stocking.

Threads to Treasure

Experienced stitchers love Lois Caron's threads. Her line of cotton, silk, and silk/wool fibers are all hand-dyed, and the colors are rich and lustrous.

    Under the name The Caron Collection, Lois has designed patterns for needlepoint and cross-stitch since 1975. But she found that stores weren't carrying the sophisticated fibers and colors she wanted to use. So in the late 1980s, she began experimenting with dyeing threads in her own kitchen.

Today, Lois has moved the business out of her kitchen and into a warehouse. It's a good thing, too, since her threads are selling well not only in the United States but also in Australia, New Zealand, and England. (For retail sources near you, see the listing on page 157.)

    The stocking ornaments on the preceding pages are Lois's designs and use her threads. Stitch them yourself, and you'll discover what her fans already know: When floss is so beautiful you hate to unwind it, the stitching is bound to be gorgeous.

Embroidery Diagrams

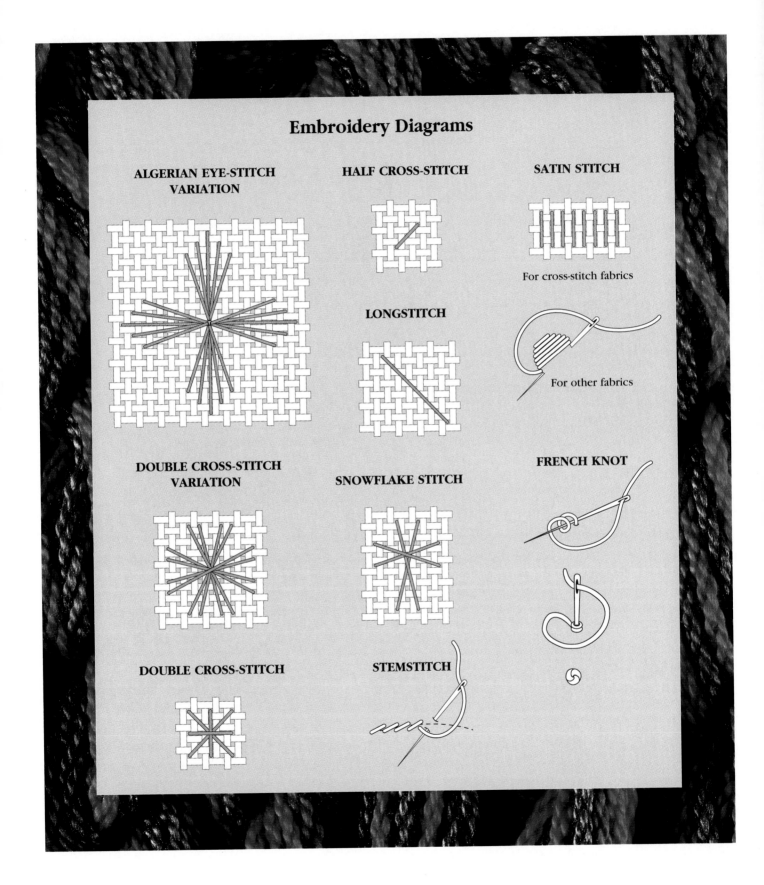

ALGERIAN EYE-STITCH VARIATION

HALF CROSS-STITCH

SATIN STITCH

For cross-stitch fabrics

LONGSTITCH

For other fabrics

DOUBLE CROSS-STITCH VARIATION

SNOWFLAKE STITCH

FRENCH KNOT

DOUBLE CROSS-STITCH

STEMSTITCH

A Tree for the Birds

Your feathered friends aren't the only ones who will enjoy a tree trimmed with birdseed ornaments and edible garlands. The decorations are fun to make and easy enough for the children to do. And the whole family will have a good time guessing who just flew in.

Birdseed Stars and Wreaths

Mix together ¾ cup flour, ½ cup water, and 3 tablespoons corn syrup. Add 4 cups birdseed and mix well.

Cover a tray with waxed paper. To make stars, place star-shaped cookie cutters on tray and spoon birdseed mixture into cookie cutters. To make wreaths, shape birdseed mixture into wreaths and place on tray; if desired, decorate wreaths with holly berries, cranberries, or raisins. Let dry for 4 to 6 hours. Remove stars from cookie cutters. Turn ornaments over and dry for an additional 4 to 6 hours. Referring to illustrations, wrap raffia around each ornament and tie a hanger loop to raffia as shown.

Birdseed Bells

For edible glue, mix together ¾ cup flour, ¼ cup water, and 3 tablespoons corn syrup. Using a paintbrush, coat 2¼"-diameter peat pots with edible glue; then roll pots in birdseed to cover. Place bells on waxed paper and let dry for 4 to 6 hours. To make a clapper for each bell, use a needle and thread to string 4 or 5 cranberries, pass needle through top of bell, and knot thread.

Referring to illustration, thread twine or raffia through drainage holes of each pot and knot at top of bell. (If pots have no holes, use an icepick to make 2 holes.) If desired, place a paper-twist or raffia bow on top and knot twine to secure. For hanger loop, knot twine again several inches from top of bell.

Dried-Fruit Wreaths

Thread a large needle, such as a darning needle, with cotton string or dental floss. Make a knot 4" to 6" from 1 end. String dried fruit (we used apricots, papaya, and raisins) until you have enough to form a small wreath; knot string together to secure circle. If desired, place a paper-twist or raffia bow on top and knot string to secure. For hanger loop, knot string tails again several inches from top of wreath.

Pretzel Garland

Thread a large needle with cotton string or dental floss. String pretzels, peanuts in shells, and dried fruit (we used pears, oranges, and limes). Add a few pinecones and sprigs of holly or pine, knotting string around these larger pieces. When garland is desired length, loop and knot each end for hanger loops.

Popcorn Garland

Pop a couple of batches of colored-kernel popcorn. Thread a large needle with cotton string or dental floss. String popped popcorn and several kinds of dried fruit (we used pineapple, oranges, and limes). When garland is desired length, loop and knot each end for hanger loops.

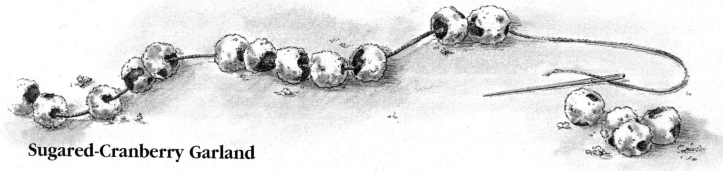

Sugared-Cranberry Garland

To make sugared cranberries, roll fresh cranberries in lightly beaten egg whites and then in superfine granulated sugar. Place cranberries on waxed paper to dry. To make garland, thread a large needle, such as a darning needle, with cotton string or dental floss. Loop and knot end for hanger loop. String cranberries until garland is desired length; then loop and knot end for hanger loop.

IDEAS

HEARTH-WARMERS

These homey projects will make cuddling up
by the fire even cozier. While you package
potpourri and pinecone fire starters for gifts,
the children can paint a cookie plate for Santa.

Pinecone Fire Starters

To use one of these wax-coated starters, light the wick, place the starter on the logs, and let the flames begin. To make 6, gather:

- 6 large pinecones
- Candle-making supplies: 6 (4") lengths wicking, 3 (1-pound) boxes paraffin, and 2 (¾-ounce) packages each cinnamon fragrance and dye (available at crafts stores)
- 1 (3-pound) coffee can
- waxed paper

Tie 1 end of wicking to the top of each pinecone. Place coffee can in a saucepan containing several inches of water. In can, melt half of the paraffin; then add 1 package each of dye and fragrance. Remove the can and let the wax cool a bit. Dip 3 pinecones several times to coat each one; then place them on waxed paper to cool. Repeat for 3 remaining pinecones. For gift giving, make fabric sacks, fill them with pinecones, and tie them off with rope.

Fireside Potpourri

This isn't your average potpourri. Toss a handful on the fire: The potpourri's fragrance intensifies while it turns the flames violet. To make 8 cups, gather:

- 3 cups evergreen clippings
- 2 cups cinnamon sticks, broken
- 1 cup each holly berries, dried orange pieces, and wood shavings
- 2 tablespoons whole cloves
- 2 teaspoons ground nutmeg
- several tiny pinecones
- 4 ounces copper sulfate (available at pharmacies)

Mix the ingredients and store in an airtight container until ready to use. Package the potpourri in cellophane gift bags. Wear gloves when handling the copper sulfate.

Santa's Cookie Plate

Buy a charger at a restaurant-supply or kitchen store. Using acrylic paints, paint a message to Santa around the rim. To ensure your hand-painted treasure will hold up for Christmases to come, wash it by hand.

PATTERNS

Quick Guide to Using the Patterns

Throughout this section you will find guidelines and tips for using the patterns.

Here is a list of helpful tools you may want to have on hand: tracing paper, carbon paper, dressmaker's carbon paper, a dressmaker's pen and chalk pencil, a water-soluble marker, a black felt-tipped permanent marker, a pencil, white and colored pencils, a ruler, scissors, and a craft knife.

Transferring Patterns to Fabric

The method you use for transferring the pattern will depend on the type of material to which the pattern is being transferred.

To transfer simple patterns to most any fabric, lay tracing paper on the printed pattern and trace. Cut out the traced pattern on the outline. Pin the pattern to the fabric and cut around the pattern.

For light-colored, lightweight fabric or paper, trace or photocopy the pattern. Retrace the outline with a black marker. Tape the tracing to a window pane or light box; then tape the material over the tracing. Using a water-soluble marker, trace the pattern onto the material.

For solid or opaque materials such as dark fabric or card-stock paper, trace the pattern. Stack the material (right side up), the carbon paper (carbon side down), and the tracing of the pattern (right side up). With a dull pencil, trace over the pattern to transfer the carbon outline to the material.

Transferring Embroidery Patterns

For embroidery patterns, there are two methods: (1) Trace the design onto tracing paper. Poke holes along the outline with a pushpin. Mark over the lines with a dressmaker's chalk pencil so chalk is imprinted on the fabric. (2) Or use a hot-iron transfer pencil to trace the pattern. Following the manufacturer's instructions, transfer the pattern onto the material.

Always transfer all placement and guide markings as well as the outline to the traced pattern and material.

Art for the Hearth

Instructions are on page 17. Patterns are full-size.

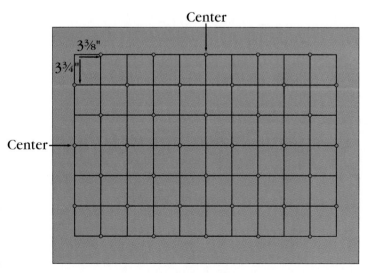

DIAGRAM 1

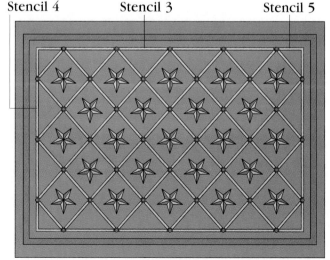

DIAGRAM 2

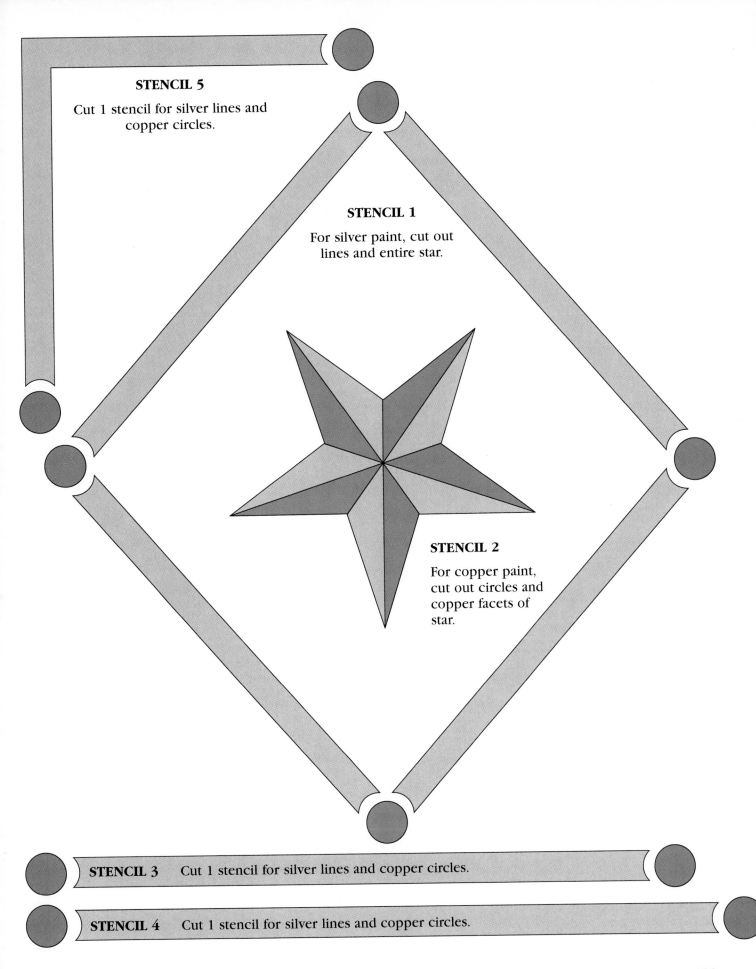

STENCIL 5

Cut 1 stencil for silver lines and copper circles.

STENCIL 1

For silver paint, cut out lines and entire star.

STENCIL 2

For copper paint, cut out circles and copper facets of star.

STENCIL 3   Cut 1 stencil for silver lines and copper circles.

STENCIL 4   Cut 1 stencil for silver lines and copper circles.

Precious Metals

Instructions begin
on page 19.
Patterns are full-size.

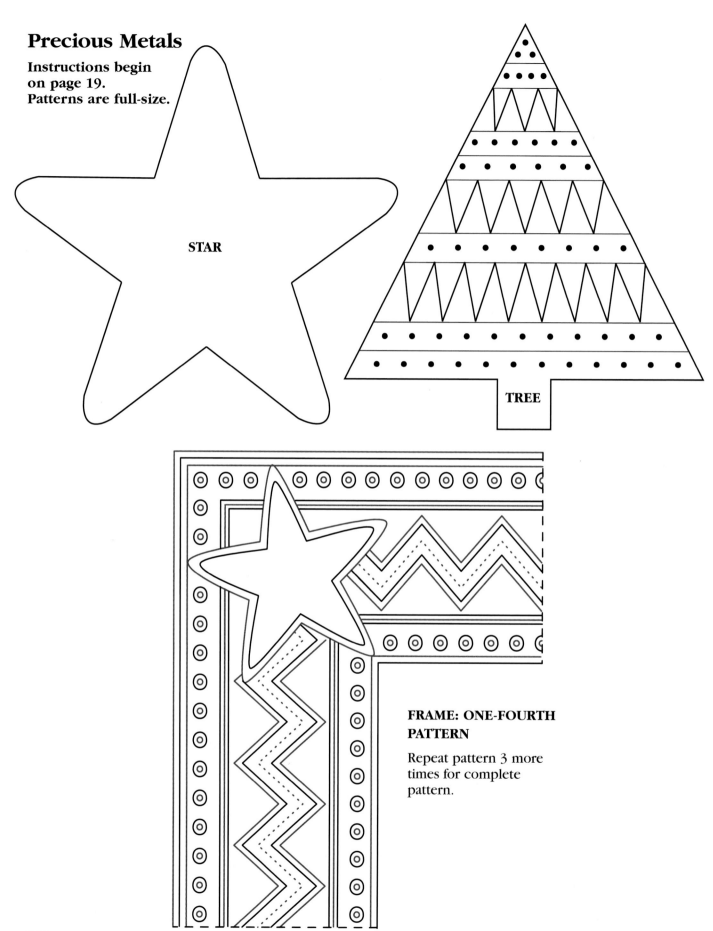

STAR

TREE

**FRAME: ONE-FOURTH
PATTERN**

Repeat pattern 3 more
times for complete
pattern.

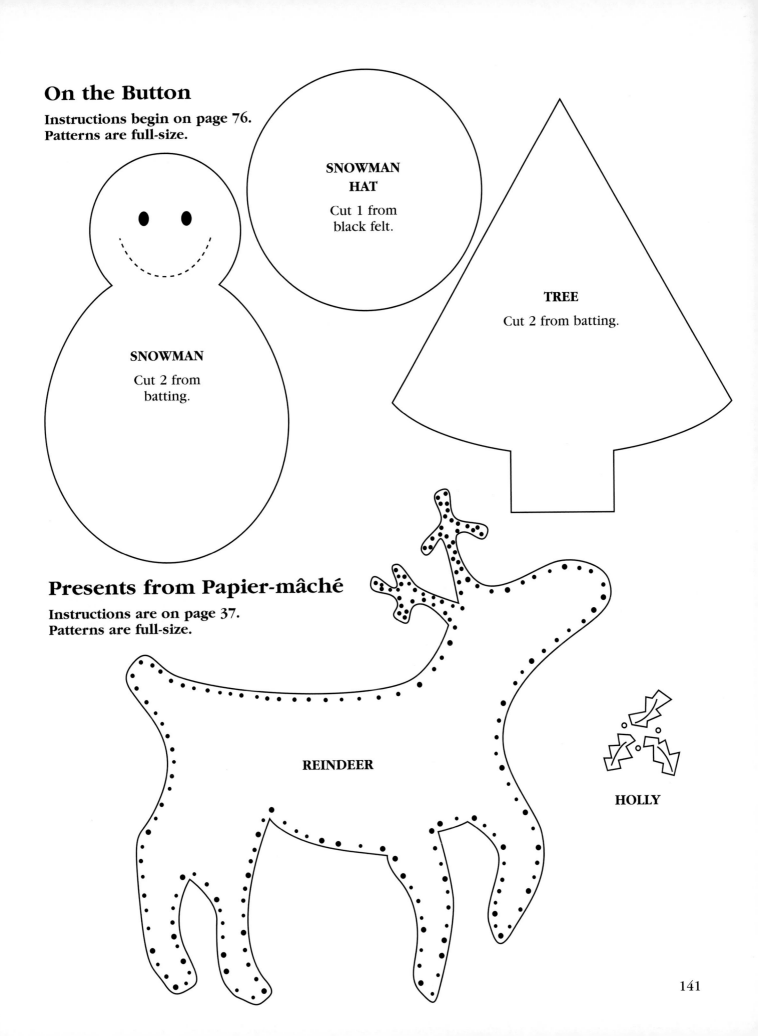

On the Button

Instructions begin on page 76.
Patterns are full-size.

**SNOWMAN
HAT**

Cut 1 from
black felt.

TREE

Cut 2 from batting.

SNOWMAN

Cut 2 from
batting.

Presents from Papier-mâché

Instructions are on page 37.
Patterns are full-size.

REINDEER

HOLLY

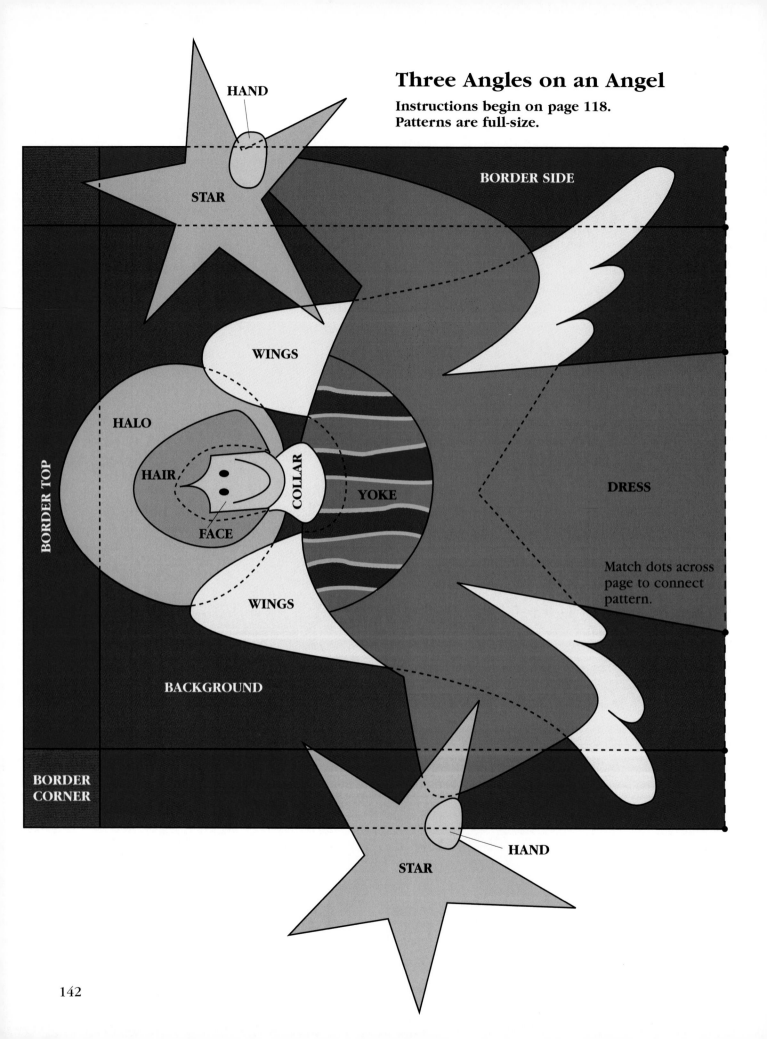

Three Angles on an Angel

Instructions begin on page 118.
Patterns are full-size.

HAND

BORDER SIDE

STAR

WINGS

HALO

HAIR

COLLAR

YOKE

DRESS

FACE

BORDER TOP

Match dots across
page to connect
pattern.

WINGS

BACKGROUND

BORDER
CORNER

HAND

STAR

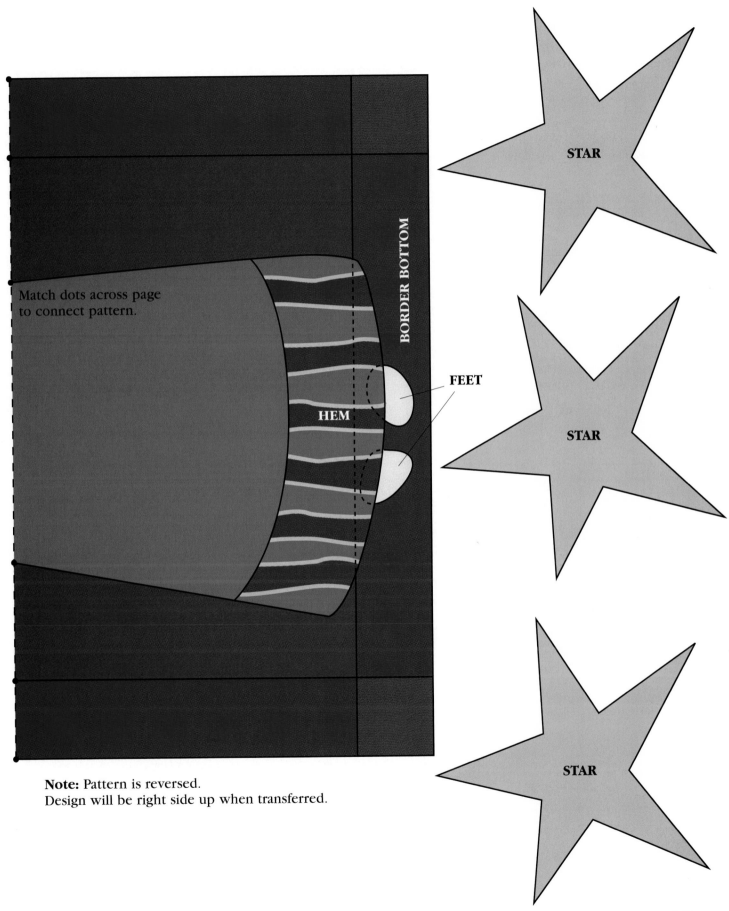

Match dots across page
to connect pattern.

BORDER BOTTOM

FEET

HEM

STAR

STAR

STAR

Note: Pattern is reversed.
Design will be right side up when transferred.

Stitch Stockings with a Flourish

Instructions begin on page 54.
Patterns are full-size. Add ¼" seam allowances to stocking patterns.

Match dots across page to connect pattern.

**STOCKING WITH
MIDDY-BRAID DESIGN**

Cut 2 from hemp canvas.

Placement lines for middy-braid design

Match dots across page
to connect pattern.

Match dots across page to connect pattern.

STOCKING WITH SOUTACHE DESIGN

Cut 2 from hemp canvas.

Placement lines for soutache design

The Velvet Touch

**Instructions begin on page 114.
Patterns are full-size.**

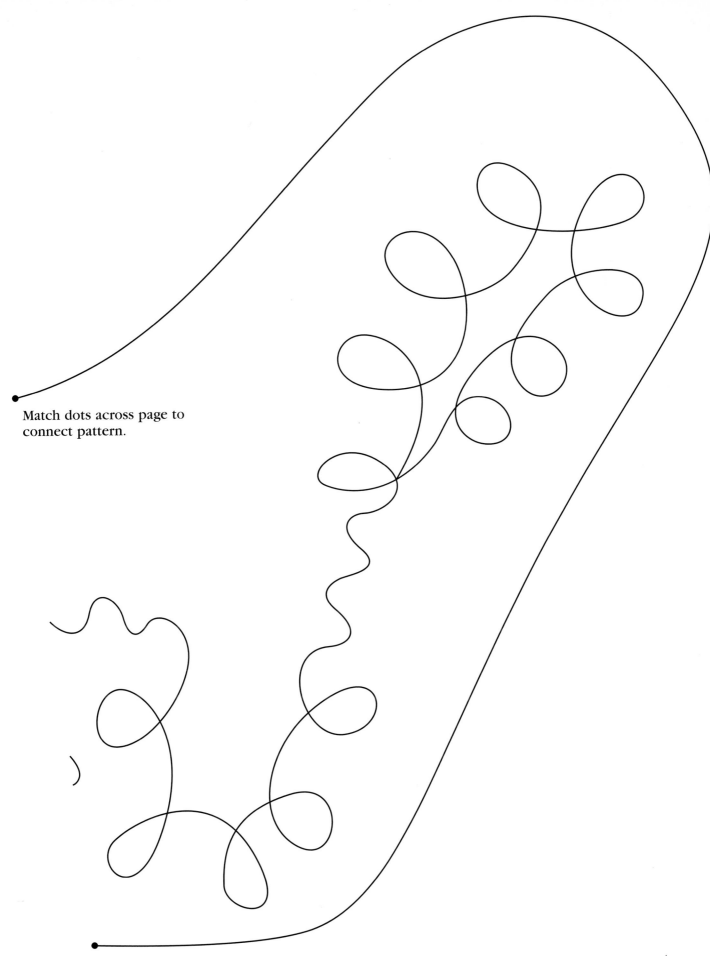

Match dots across page to
connect pattern.

Monkey Business

Instructions begin on page 78.
Patterns are full-size and include ¼" seam allowances.

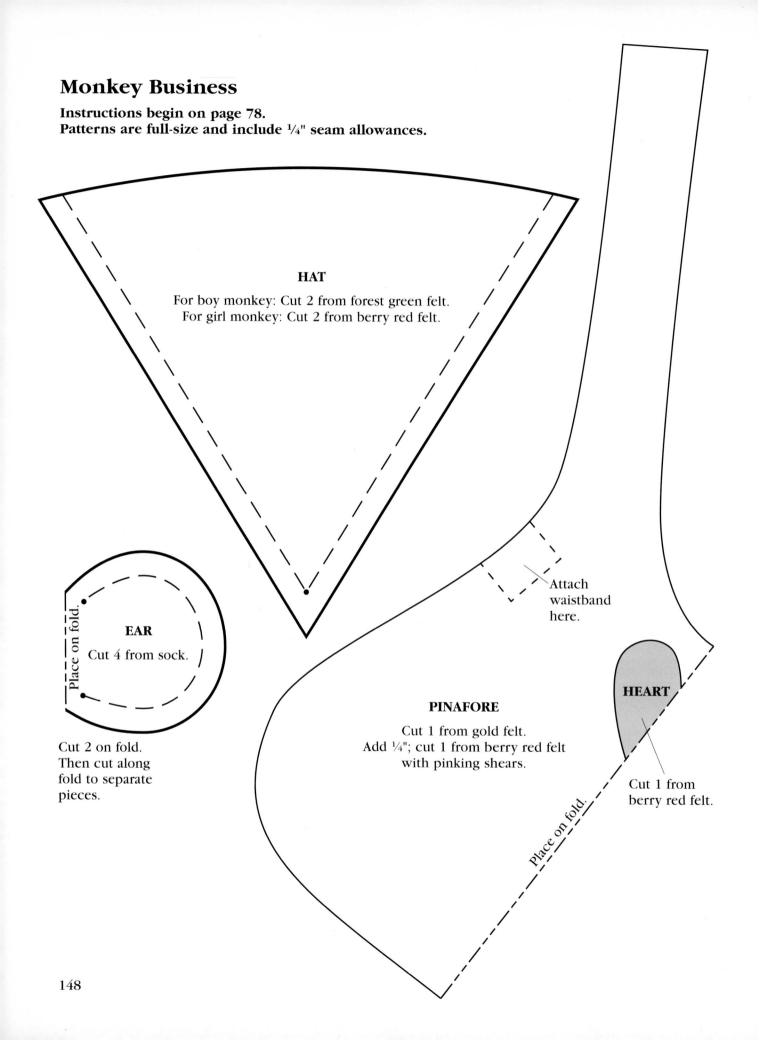

HAT

For boy monkey: Cut 2 from forest green felt.
For girl monkey: Cut 2 from berry red felt.

EAR

Cut 4 from sock.

Place on fold.

Cut 2 on fold.
Then cut along
fold to separate
pieces.

Attach
waistband
here.

PINAFORE

Cut 1 from gold felt.
Add ¼"; cut 1 from berry red felt
with pinking shears.

Place on fold.

HEART

Cut 1 from
berry red felt.

148

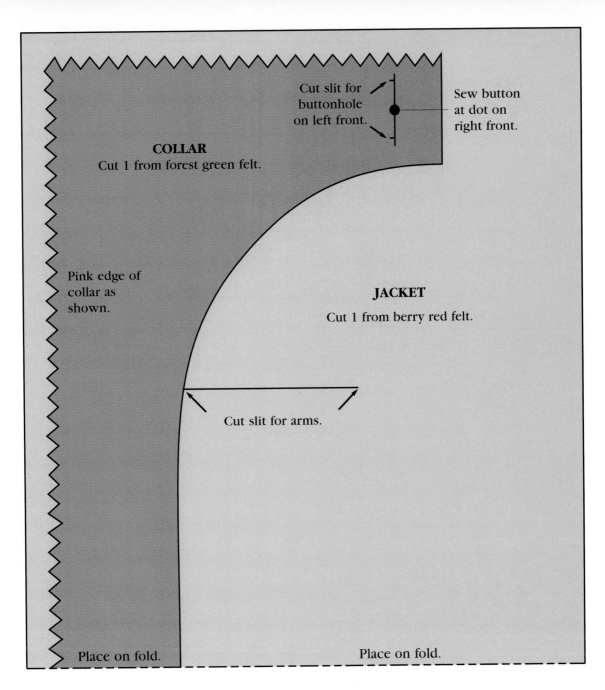

COLLAR
Cut 1 from forest green felt.

Cut slit for buttonhole on left front.

Sew button at dot on right front.

Pink edge of collar as shown.

JACKET
Cut 1 from berry red felt.

Cut slit for arms.

Place on fold.

Place on fold.

Note: See page 131 for embroidery diagrams.

EMBROIDERY PATTERN FOR GIRL MONKEY

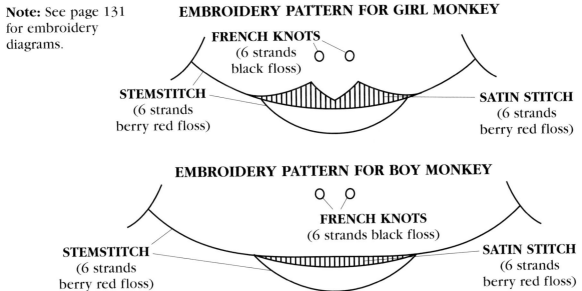

FRENCH KNOTS
(6 strands black floss)

STEMSTITCH
(6 strands berry red floss)

SATIN STITCH
(6 strands berry red floss)

EMBROIDERY PATTERN FOR BOY MONKEY

FRENCH KNOTS
(6 strands black floss)

STEMSTITCH
(6 strands berry red floss)

SATIN STITCH
(6 strands berry red floss)

Wee Three Stockings

Instructions begin on page 128.

Note:. Each square of chart represents 2 threads of fabric. For number of strands to use, see color key.

Snowflake Stocking

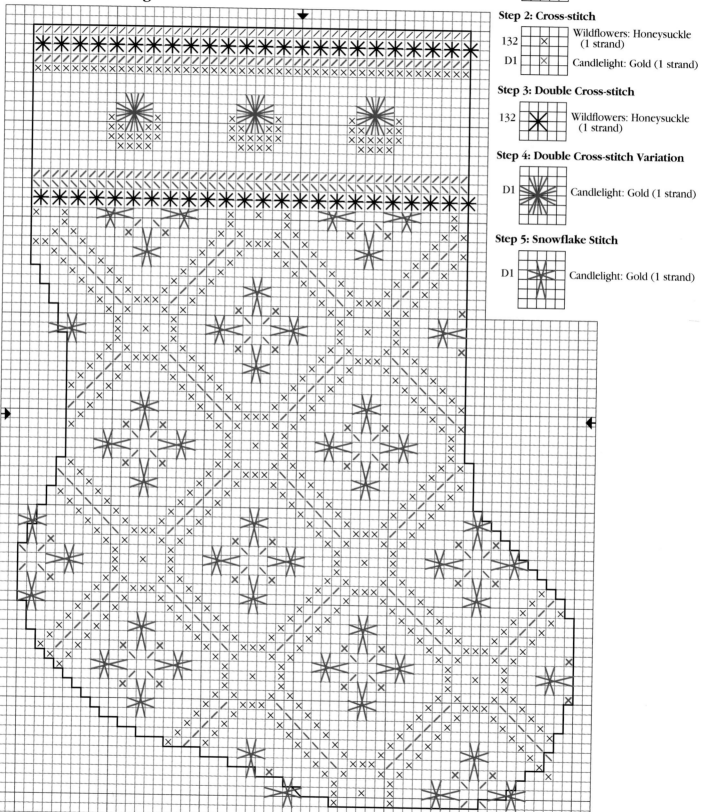

Step 1: Half Cross-stitch

132 — Wildflowers: Honeysuckle (1 strand)
D1 — Candlelight: Gold (1 strand)
D1 — Candlelight: Gold (1 strand)

Step 2: Cross-stitch

132 — Wildflowers: Honeysuckle (1 strand)
D1 — Candlelight: Gold (1 strand)

Step 3: Double Cross-stitch

132 — Wildflowers: Honeysuckle (1 strand)

Step 4: Double Cross-stitch Variation

D1 — Candlelight: Gold (1 strand)

Step 5: Snowflake Stitch

D1 — Candlelight: Gold (1 strand)

Flying Colors Stocking

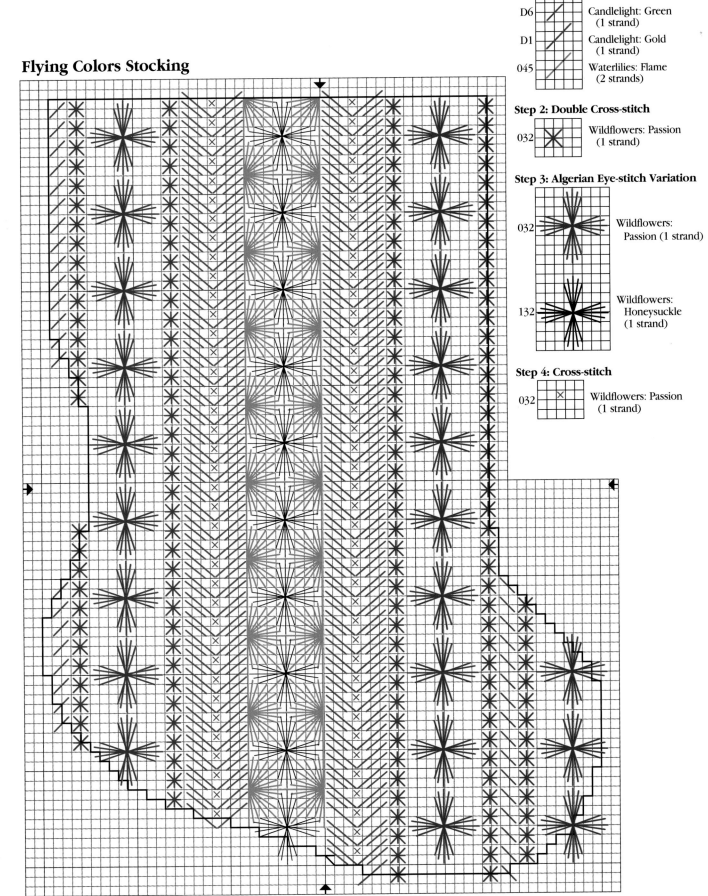

Step 1: Longstitch

D6		Candlelight: Green (1 strand)
D1		Candlelight: Gold (1 strand)
045		Waterlilies: Flame (2 strands)

Step 2: Double Cross-stitch

032		Wildflowers: Passion (1 strand)

Step 3: Algerian Eye-stitch Variation

032		Wildflowers: Passion (1 strand)
132		Wildflowers: Honeysuckle (1 strand)

Step 4: Cross-stitch

032		Wildflowers: Passion (1 strand)

151

Winter Forest Stocking

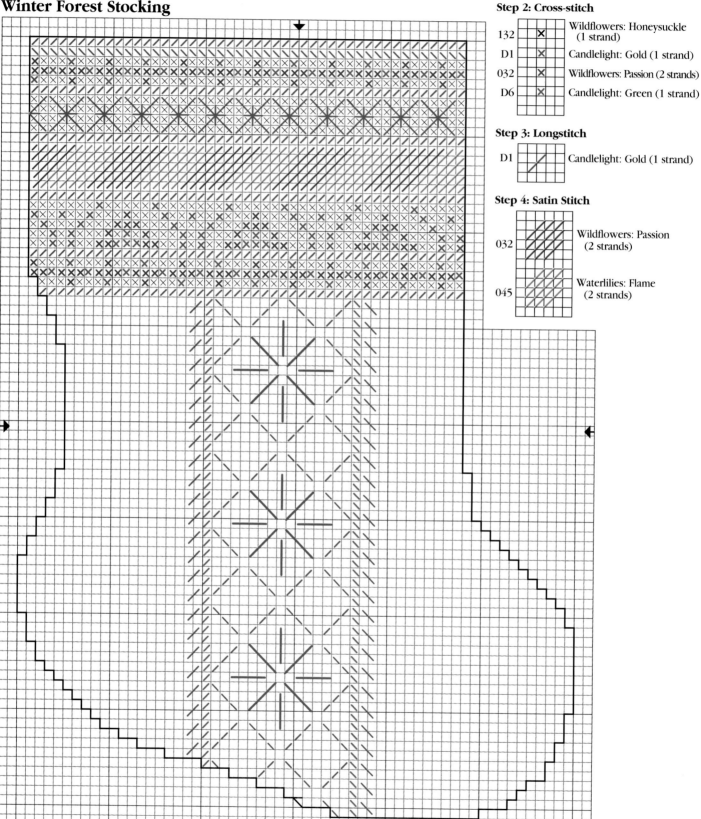

Step 1: Half Cross-stitch

D1	/	Candlelight: Gold (1 strand)
D6	/	Candlelight: Green (1 strand)

Step 2: Cross-stitch

132	✕	Wildflowers: Honeysuckle (1 strand)
D1	✕	Candlelight: Gold (1 strand)
032	✕	Wildflowers: Passion (2 strands)
D6	✕	Candlelight: Green (1 strand)

Step 3: Longstitch

D1		Candlelight: Gold (1 strand)

Step 4: Satin Stitch

032		Wildflowers: Passion (2 strands)
045		Waterlilies: Flame (2 strands)

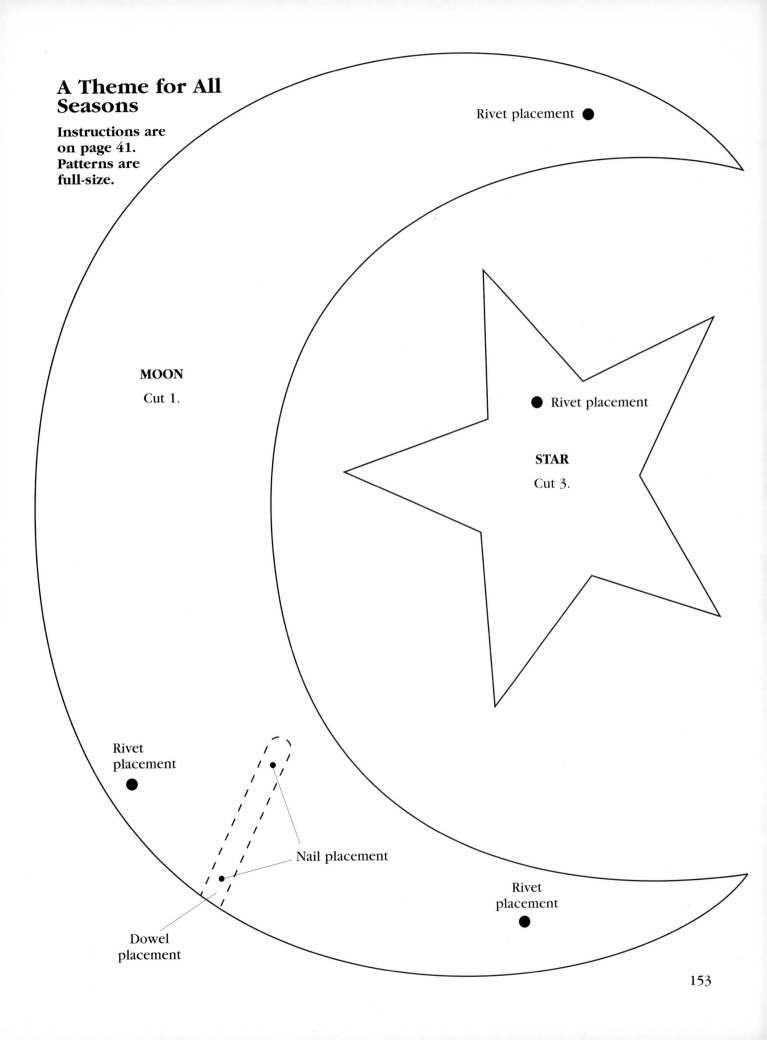

A Theme for All Seasons

Instructions are
on page 41.
Patterns are
full-size.

Rivet placement ●

MOON

Cut 1.

● Rivet placement

STAR

Cut 3.

Rivet
placement
●

Nail placement

Rivet
placement
●

Dowel
placement

153

Perches with Perfect Pitch

Instructions are on page 9.
Patterns are full-size.

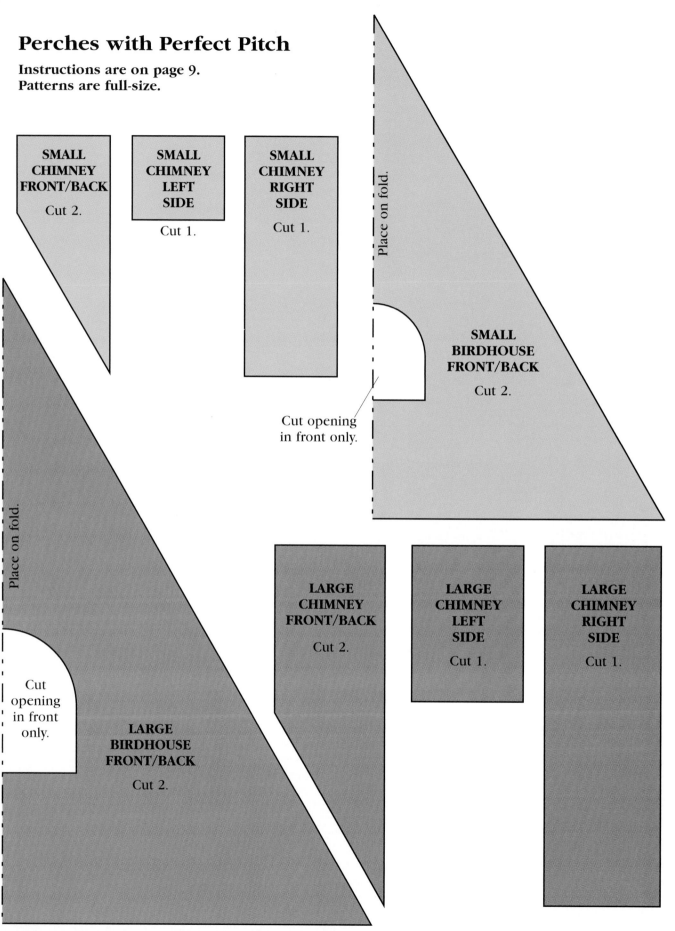

SMALL
CHIMNEY
FRONT/BACK

Cut 2.

SMALL
CHIMNEY
LEFT
SIDE

Cut 1.

SMALL
CHIMNEY
RIGHT
SIDE

Cut 1.

Place on fold.

SMALL
BIRDHOUSE
FRONT/BACK

Cut 2.

Cut opening
in front only.

Place on fold.

Cut
opening
in front
only.

LARGE
BIRDHOUSE
FRONT/BACK

Cut 2.

LARGE
CHIMNEY
FRONT/BACK

Cut 2.

LARGE
CHIMNEY
LEFT
SIDE

Cut 1.

LARGE
CHIMNEY
RIGHT
SIDE

Cut 1.

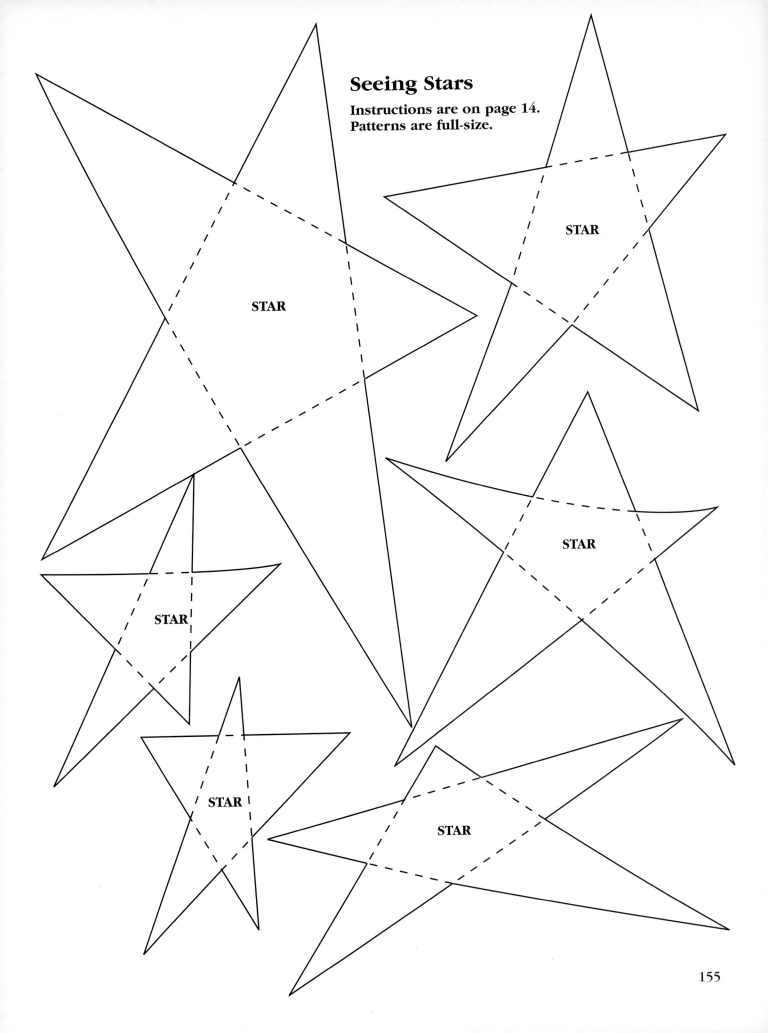

Seeing Stars
Instructions are on page 14.
Patterns are full-size.

STAR

STAR

STAR

STAR

STAR

STAR

SOURCES

• Page 11—For information on Beauregard, contact the shop at 19 S. Block St., Fayetteville, AR 72701; or call (501) 521-2592.

• Page 12—raffia: For catalog, send $4 to Loose Ends, P.O. Box 20310, Salem, OR 97307; or call (503) 390-7457.

Fimo clay

evergreen garland: For fresh trees, wreaths, and garlands by mail, contact JBC Tree Farm, 318 Touhy Ave., Park Ridge, IL 60068; or call (800) 540-3391.

birdhouses, garden angel: L. Pizitz & Co., P.O. Box 4670, Seaside, FL 32459; or call (904) 231-2281.

• Page 17—custom-designed floorcloths: Molly Pritchett Designs, P.O. Box 55, Libertytown, MD 21762; or call (301) 898-3757. Send $2 for brochure.

• Page 21—craft metal: St. Louis Crafts, Inc., 7606 Idaho Ave., St. Louis, MO 63111-3219; or call (800) 841-7631.

• Page 23—flag fabric, flagpoles: Send $2 for catalog to Kite Studio, 5555 Hamilton Blvd., Wescoville, PA 18106; or call (800) KITE-991 or (610) 395-3560.

• Pages 25-27—pillow fabrics: stripe, Belvedere Stripe by Schumacher, 79 Madison Ave., New York, NY 10016; or call consumer referral service at (800) 332-3384.

check fabric: Langham Check by Colefax and Fowler, available through designers from Cowtan & Tout, 979 Third Ave., New York, NY 10022; or call (212) 753-4488.

• Page 33—birch bark: For catalog, send $1 to Colorado Evergreen, 255 S.W. 42nd, Loveland, CO 80537; or call (970) 667-3770.

birch-bark paper: For catalog, write to MPR Associates, Inc., P.O. Box 7343, High Point, NC 27264; or call (800) 454-3331.

• Page 38—Nancy Thomas Studio Gallery, P.O. Box 274, Yorktown, VA 23690; or call (804) 898-3665. Send $2 for catalog.

• Page 49—Fimo clay, jewelry findings: For catalog, write to TSI, Inc., P.O. Box 9266, Seattle, WA 98109; or call (800) 426-9984.

• Page 53—corrugated cardboard, trims: For catalog, send $4 to Loose Ends, P.O. Box 20310, Salem, OR 97307; or call (503) 390-7457.

• Pages 54 and 55—hemp canvas: For wholesale price list, contact Hands All Around, 1609 8th Ave. S.W., Olympia, WA 98502; or call (206) 357-7703.

trims: G Street Fabrics, 11854 Rockville Pike, Rockville, MD 20852; or call (800) 333-9191.

• Page 63—reproduction and unfinished game boards, playing pieces: Games People Played, P.O. Box 1540, Pinedale, WY 82941; or call (307) 367-2502. For catalog of reproduction boards, send $3.50.

Santa by
Nancy Thomas

Reproduction game board

• Page 65—45-count linen by Zweigart: contact Needleworker's Delight, 100 Claridge Pl., Colonia, NJ 07067; or call (800) 931-4545 for free catalog.

handkerchiefs: Vermont Country Store, P.O. Box 3000, Manchester Center, VT 05255; or call (802) 362-2400.

• Page 69—handmade and specialty papers: For a catalog, send $4 to Loose Ends, P.O. Box 20310, Salem, OR 97307; or call (503) 390-7457.

ribbon: Midori, Inc., 1432 Elliott Ave. W., Seattle, WA 98102. For information on stores carrying Midori ribbon, call (800) 659-3049.

sealing wax, stamp "metal ring": Victorian Papers, P.O. Box 411341, Kansas City, MO 64141-1341; or call (800) 800-6647. For catalog, send $2, redeemable toward purchase.

rubber stamps: For catalog, send $4 to Stamp Francisco, 466 8th Street, San Francisco, CA 94103; or call (415) 252-5975.

• Page 70—patina: For free catalog, contact Modern Options, 2325 Third St., Suite 339, San Francisco, CA 94107; or call (415) 252-5580.

• Page 76—cotton batting: Warm Products, Inc., 16110 Woodinville-Redmond Rd. #4, Woodinville, WA 98072. Send SASE for sample, brochure, and list of retailers.

Clay beads

buttons by the pound: Buttons and Things, 24 Main St., Route 1, Freeport, ME 04032; or call (207) 865-4480.

• Pages 78 and 81—ragg socks: J. Crew, Inc., One Ivy Crescent, Lynchburg, VA 24513-2001; or call (800) 562-0258.

wool felt: For free catalog, contact Central/Shippee, Inc., P.O. Box 135, Bloomingdale, NJ 07403; or call (800) 631-8968.

red-heeled sock monkey kits: Vermont Country Store, P.O. Box 3000, Manchester Center, VT 05255; or call (802) 362-2400.

• Page 81—Jamondas Press: For storybooks (which include patterns for sock animals) and red-heeled socks, contact Jamondas Press, P.O. Box 3325, Ann Arbor, MI 48106; or call (800) 223-7873.

• Page 83—mittens: For free catalog, contact Hanna Andersson, 1010 N.W. Flanders, Portland, OR 97209; or call (800) 222-0544.

• Page 89—ribbon candy: Hammond Candy Co., 2550 West 29th Ave., Denver, CO 80211; or call (303) 455-2320.

• Page 98—glass gems: For free catalog, contact HearthSong, 6519 N. Galena Road, Peoria, IL 61656; or call (800) 325-2502.

• Page 100—striped tablecloth, plaid and jacquard dish towels: For a retail source near you, contact TAG, Ltd., 1730 W. Wrightwood, Chicago, IL 60614.

• Page 106—spices and spice jars: For free catalog, contact Spices, Etc., P.O. Box 5266, Charlottesville, VA 22905; or call (800) 827-6373.

spices and spice jars: For free catalog, contact Penzeys Spice, Ltd., P.O. Box 1448, Waukesha, WI 53186; or call (414) 574-0277, fax (414) 574-0278.

Design and fabrics by Patrick Lose

rubber stamps: For catalog, send $4 to Stamp Francisco, 466 8th St., San Francisco, CA 94103; or call (415) 252-5975.

• Page 115—velvet, trim: G Street Fabrics, 11854 Rockville Pike, Rockville, MD 20852; or call (800) 333-9191.

• Page 121—Patrick Lose patterns: Out on a Whim, P.O. Box 65156, West Des Moines, IA 50265.

Patrick Lose fabrics: United Notions and Fabrics, 13795 Hutton, Dallas TX 75234; or call (214) 484-8901.

• Page 123—soap-making kits, essential oils: For catalog, send $2 to Sunfeather Soap Company, 1551 State Hwy. 72, Potsdam, NY 13676; or call (800) 771-7627.

essential oils, castile soap: Caswell-Massey Co., Ltd., 121 Fieldcrest Ave., Edison, NJ 08837; or call (800) 326-0500.

• Pages 128 and 130—For information on shops carrying The Caron Collection threads, contact The Caron Collection, 67 Poland St., Bridgeport, CT 06605; or call (203) 333-0325.

28-count linen by Wichelt Imports: For catalog, send $3 to Universal Stitcher, P.O. Box 581726, Minneapolis, MN 55458-1726; or call (800) 830-5027, fax (612) 825-1161.

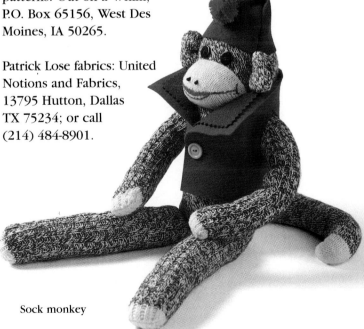

Sock monkey

INDEX

GENERAL

RECIPES

CONTRIBUTORS

DESIGNERS

Leslie Batchelor, hemp stockings, 54-55.

Lois Caron, embroidered ornaments, 128-31.

Kay Clark, craft metal projects, 18, 20-21.

Janice Cox, bath salts, soaps, oils, 122-27

Janet R. Farris, bead star ornament, 50.

Chris Goddard, door garland, 10-12.

Amanda Hagood, Santa's cookie plate, 137.

Charlotte Hagood, sock monkey dolls, 79, 80; velvet designs, 110-13, 115.

Deby Harvey, tabletop trees, 71-73.

Becky Havekost, watercolors of tree designs, 71.

Diana Hedlund, twig swag, 14-15.

Margot Hotchkiss, mittens, 82-83.

Angie Howard, bead designs, 44-51.

Lori A. Kennedy, birch-bark wreath, 30-31, 32; pinecone fire starters and plaid bags, 136-37.

Heidi T. King, papier-mâché projects, 34-37; rope stamp cards, 42-43; cotton-batting tree skirt and ornaments, 74-75, 77.

Patrick Lose, fabrics, 116-17, 121; three angel designs, star pins, 118-21.

Molly Pritchett, hearth rug, 16.

Janice Schindeler, Twice as Nice recipes, 66-69; Spice Blends, 102.

Betsy Scott, birdhouses, 6-7, 8; tree for the birds, 132, 135.

Sarah Stahlie, gift bags by Loose Ends, 52.

Elizabeth Taliaferro, Visions of Sugarplums recipes, 86-91; Wine and Cheese Buffet, 92-97; Sweets in Seconds recipes, 108-9.

Nancy Thomas, tin tree topper, 40-41.

Mary Thompson, checkerboard, 58-63.

Carol Tipton, marble projects, 56-57; fireside pot-pourri, 136-37.

Cynthia M. Wheeler, outdoor flag, 22; botanical handkerchiefs, 64-65; tablecloth, 101.

Peggy Ann Williams, pillow slipcovers, 24-27.

PHOTOGRAPHERS

All photographs except the following were taken by **John O'Hagan.**

Ralph Anderson, 44-51, 66, 68-69, 74-77, 81, 86-91, 92-97, 102-7, 108-9, 122-27, left 156.

Jim Bathie, inset 29.

Rick Dean, inset 6-7, 22, inset 30-31, 32, inset 58-59, 70, 72-73, inset 84-85, inset 110-11, 132, 135.

Keith Harrelson, background 30-31, 42-43, 79-80, 82-83, 101, background 110-11, silhouettes, 120-21, right 156, center 157.

Mary-Gray Hunter, 20.

Gene Johnson, 10-12.

Ariel Skelley, 38-41, bottom 156.

PHOTO STYLISTS

All photographs except the following were styled by **Katie Stoddard.**

Virginia R. Cravens, 66, 68-69, 86-91, 92-97, 102-7, 108-9.

Tova Cubert, inset 6-7, 22, inset 30-31, 32, inset 58-59, 70, 72-73, inset 84-85, inset 110-11, 132, 135.

Nancy Ingram, 10-12.

SPECIAL THANKS

• Thanks to the following talented people:

Elizabeth Andress
Marilynn Arm
Christy and Lindsey Armstrong
Anita Bice
Carol O. Loria
Susan Reynolds

• Thanks to the following homeowners:

Kris Childs, Birmingham, AL
Jack Crouch, Birmingham, AL
Bryan and Allyson Hunt, Springdale, AR
Nancy and Carl Jernigan, Birmingham, AL
Tom and Elizabeth Jernigan, Birmingham, AL
Donna and Bob Martin, Des Moines, IA
Kit Samford, Birmingham, AL

• Thanks to the following businesses:

Alabama Art Supply, Birmingham, AL
Classic Wine Company, Birmingham, AL
Finely Finished Needlepoint, East Haddam, CT
MGTI, Birmingham, AL